The Danes in Lancashire

D1357552

Canute.

The Danes in Lancashire

BY

S. W. PARTINGTON

ILLUSTRATED

DIDSBURY MANCHESTER
ENGLAND

First Published 1909
SHERRATT & HUGHES
33 Soho Square, London
34 Cross Street, Manchester

08467411 L000296392
03056488

Republished 1973
E. J. MORTEN (Publishers)
10 Warburton Street, Didsbury
Manchester, England

ISBN 0 85972 000 4

Printed in Great Britain by
The Scolar Press Limited, Menston, Yorkshire

PREFACE.

THE story of the 'childhood of our race' who inhabited the counties of Lancashire and Yorkshire before the Norman Conquest, is an almost blank page to the popular reader of to-day. The last invaders of our shores, whom we designate as the Danes and Norsemen, were not the least important of our ancestors. The History of their daring adventures, crafts and customs, beliefs and character, with the surviving traces in our language and laws, form the subject of this book.

From the evidence of relics, and of existing customs and traditions, we trace their thought and actions, their first steps in speech and handicraft, and the development of their religious conceptions. Our education authorities have realized the fact that "Local Names" contain a fund of history and meaning which appeals to the young as well as to the adults; and the county committees have been well advised to recommend the teaching of History and Geography from local features and events.

Some articles written by the late Mr. John Just, M.A., of Bury, on our early races, and elements of our language and dialect, formed the incentive to the writer to continue the story of our Danish ancestors.

To the following writers we are indebted for many facts and quotations: H. Colley March, Esq., M.D.; W. G. Collingwood, "Scandinavian Britain"; W. S. Calverley, "Stone Crosses and Monuments of Westmorland and Cumberland"; Dr. W. Wagner's "Tales and Traditions of our Northern Ancestors"; Mr. Boyle, "Danes in the East Riding of Yorkshire"; Mr. J. W. Bradley, B.A., of the Salt Museum, Stafford, "Runic Calendars and Clog-Almanacs"; Rev. J. Hay Colligan, Liverpool; Professor W. A. Herdman, Liverpool; Mr. Jas. T. Marquis, of the Battle of "Brunanburh"; Dr. Worsäac, "Danes in England."

Messrs. Titus Wilson & Son, Kendal, Plates, "Map of Races," etc.; Swan, Sonnenschein & Co., London; Williams, Norgate & Co., London.

To Charles W. Sutton, Esq., Free Reference Library, Manchester, for valuable advice and assistance grateful thanks are now tendered.

S. W. PARTINGTON.

BURY, *October 4, 1909.*

CONTENTS.

	PAGE
Invasion and Conquest	1
Settlements	11
Place-Names	45
Patronymics	59
Physical Types still existing	77
Political Freemen	87
Husbandry	109
Stone Crosses	117
Runes	135
Memorials	161
Literature	167
Mythology	187
Superstitions	203
Agriculture	213

LIST OF ILLUSTRATIONS.

Canute - - - - - *Frontispiece*

PAGE

Viking Settlements - - - - - - 13

Extwistle Hall - - - - - - - 34

Brunanburh Map - - - - - - 36

Old Dane's House - - - - - - 40

Ancient Danish Loom - - - 80

Heysham Hogback - - - - - - 120

Danish Ornaments, Claughton-on-brock - 124

Halton Cross - - - - - - - 125

Ormside Cup - - - - - - - 131

Clog Almanac Symbols - - - - - 144

Runic Calendar - - - - - - - 155

Carved Wood, with Runes - - - - 170

Bractaetes - - - - - - - - 174

Halton Cup - - - - - - - 176

Calderstones, No. I. - - - - - - 184

Calderstones, No. II. - - - - - 185

Invasion and Conquest

CHAPTER I.

Invasion and Conquest.

A victorious people have always a wide-spreading influence over the people subdued by them. An inferior race never withstood a superior one. The very fact that the Danes gained not only an ascendancy in many parts of England during the Anglo-Saxon dynasties, but even the government of them all, is a proof that they were at that period a race of individuals superior to the natives of the land. The indigenous Britons felt the ameliorating influence of the Roman superiority and the civilisation which formed an element of the Roman sway. The Danes exercised and maintained an influence equal to the extent of their amalgamation for the general good of the country. The Romans were as much superior to the aboriginal Britons as the English of the present day are to the Africans and Sikhs. The Saxons were an advance on the Romanised Celt, while on the Saxons again, the Danes or Northmen were an advance in superiority and a great element of improvement. Leaving the Danes to tell their own tale and write their own histories in favour of their own fatherland, we undertake to sketch out their connection with our own county of Lancaster, with the permanent, and still existing, effects of that connection. Hitherto history has unfolded nothing as to the date when the "Vikings" first visited the Lancashire coast, plundering the county, and slaughtering the inhabitants. The Danes first visited the eastern coasts about the year A.D. 787, as narrated in the Saxon Chronicle. In the year 894 the city of Chester fell into their hands, under the redoubtable Hastings. This celebrated place the Danes fortified, and henceforward, along with the other cities of Derby, across the island, held at intervals until their power waned by the amalgamation which eventually constituted one people. Local names are the beacon lights of primeval history. The names of places, even at this remote period of time, suffice to prove that the Danes left an impression of superiority by their invasion. At this time the Danes invaded the coast of Lancashire, and formed settlements therein. Cumberland and Westmorland were under the dominion of Cumbrian Britons. At this early period the Danes have so intermingled with the Anglo-Saxons, as to influence the names of the hundreds into which the shire was sub-divided. No chronicle may register this fact, but the words do, and will do, so long as they constitute the signs and symbols of ideas and things. The northern hundred of the shire was named Lonsdale, and extended not only over the district of Lunesdale, but also included the territory north of the sands. The second hundred into which the shire was divided was Amounderness. If we allow "ness" to be of strictly Scandinavian origin, then this hundred has a strictly Danish or Norse name, "Amounder" being the first Viking who settled in the Fylde country. Blackburn, pronounced "Blakeburn," is the third name of a hundred which lies more inland, but having little or no coast line within the shire. Inland the Scandinavian influence diminished. Hence the genuine Anglo-Saxon name of this division; in the early times "Blagburnshire." The fourth hundred is that of Salford, also inland, hence under no Danish influence. The name is genuine Anglo-Saxon and perhaps this hundred includes natives less mixed with Scandinavian population than any other in the north of England. The broad Anglo-Saxon frame is seen to perfection in the country districts, and the light, ruddy complexion. The men were made for endurance and slow in movements. It would be a difficult task to get them to move if they felt disinclined to do so. The last hundred has much sea coast, and came therefore much under Danish influence. Hence the name, West Derby Hundred. No one who knows anything of our early history will hesitate to pronounce this name altogether Danish, so that three out of the five hundreds into which the county was apportioned were under Danish domination. "Bi," Danish, in modern English "by," was the common term given by Danish settlers to their residence. Derby or Deorby means not the residence or home of the deer, but a locality where the animals abounded. The Danes had, more than any other people, a reverence for the dead. Wherever a hero fell, even if but a short time sufficed to cover his remains, this was done; and if nothing better to mark the spot, a boat which brought him hither was placed over him, keel uppermost. Failing a boat, a "Haugr" or mound was raised over his grave. When Christianity upset these "Hofs," or sacred enclosures of Odin and Thor, then crosses were erected over the Christian graves. This accounts for the universal number of "Crosbys" in the Danish district of the kingdom. Conquered Rome converted and conquered its barbarian and heathen masters to the Cross. Anglo-Saxon converted his Danish neighbour, and subdued him to the Cross. The higher the superstitions of the Pagan the greater the devotee when he is converted.

When the Danes were converted to Christianity by their intercourse with the Anglo-Saxons they transferred all their superstitious feeling to the emblems of Christianity. Churches were also built by the naturalised Danes in all places where they settled; and just as easy as it is to recognise their dwellings by their "bys," so it is to know the places where they reared their churches. Their name for a church was "kirkja." Hence in whatever compound name this word enters as a component, there it indicates a Danish origin. Hence Kirkby, Formby, Ormskirk, and Kirkdale are places appertaining to the early

Anglo-Danish history. Dale is likewise a genuine appellative, as in Kirkdale as already noticed. Besides, in this hundred we find: Skelmersdale, Ainsdale, Cuerdale, and Birkdale. The only two places which the Danes seem to have noticed in their navigation of the Ribble were Walton-le-dale and the more important Cuerdale, now renowned in archæology for the richest find of ancient coins recorded in history. The Danes brought a treasure of 7,000 pieces to Cuerdale. Mingled with the coins were bars of silver, amulets, broken rings, and ornaments of various kinds, such as are recorded by Scandinavian Sagas. Many countries had been rifled for this treasure. Kufic, Italian, Byzantine, French, and Anglo-Saxon coins were in the booty; besides 3,000 genuine Danish pieces, minted by kings and jarls on the Continent. Another discovery of Danish treasure was made at Harkirke, near Crosby. The coins here found were of a more recent deposit, and contained but one of Canute the Great. From the Mersey to the Ribble was a long, swampy, boggy plain, and was not worth the Romans' while to make roads or to fix stations or tenements. From the Conquest until the beginning of the 18th century this district was almost stagnant, and its surface undisturbed. The Dane kept to the shore, the sea was his farm. He dredged the coast and the estuary, with his innate love of danger, till Liverpool sprang up with the magic of Eastern fable, and turned out many a rover to visit every region of the world. The race of the Viking are, many of them, the richest merchants of the earth's surface.*

About half of England—the so-called "Danelag," or community of Danes, was for centuries subject to Danish laws. These laws existed for 200 years after the Norman Conquest. The Normans long retained a predilection for old Danish institutions and forms of judicature, and their new laws bear the impress and colour of the older time. This is established beyond doubt, in spite of the boast of the famous Sir Robert Peel in Parliament, that he was proud "The Danes tried in vain to overcome the institutions of England instead of securing them."

The English word "by-law" is still used to denote municipal or corporate law, which is derived from the Danish "By-Lov." This shows they must have had some share in developing the system of judicature in English cities. The "Hustings" were well known in the seven cities under Danish rule.

The earliest positive traces of a "jury" in England appear in the "Danelag," among the Danes established there; and that long before the time of William the Conqueror. The present village of Thingwall, in Cheshire, was a place of meeting for the "Thing" or "Trithing," a court held in the open air to settle laws and disputes in the same manner as that existing at Tynwald, Isle of Man.

* From an article by the late John Just, M.A., of Bury.

The division of "Ridings" in Yorkshire is also derived from this Danish custom.

The "Trithing" was a Danish institution, so also was the wapentake. What are called "hundreds" in some counties, are called "wapentakes" in others, thus from the Norse "taka," which means a "weapon grasping." Tacitus says the ancients used to "express assent by waving or brandishing their weapons." If the sentence pleased they struck their spears together, "since the most honourable kind of assent is to applaud with arms." From this practice the word came to mean the sentence or decree had been thus authenticated. "Vapantak" in the grafas of Icelandic parliament means the breaking up of the session, when the men resumed their weapons which had been laid aside during the assembly. (Cleasby.)

Local Names.

As a maritime race the Danes brought to our county not only a knowledge of the sea, how to navigate its perils, and the secret of successful trading, but also possessed the art and craft of shipbuilding to a higher degree than any then known. We still have the old Danish name in Liverpool of David Rollo and Sons, shipbuilders and engineers. The following Danish maritime terms have become part of our language: Vrag, a wreck; flaade, fleet; vinde, windlass; skibsborde, shipboard; mast, mast; seile, sails; styrmand, steersman.

From the fact that "Thingwall" in Cheshire and "Tynwald" in the Isle of Man afford the memorial of the assizes, and that "wald" or "vold" signifies a "bank" or "rampart," where these courts were held in order to be safe from surprise, may we not presume the local name "The Wylde," in Bury, to be derived from the same source, as the "bank" or "rampart" would be used previous to the building of the old castle? The Danish "byr," or "by," means a settlement, town, or village, and as the word "berg" means a hill, and "borough," "bury," "brow," and "burgh" are similar terms for a fortified hill, we may suppose "Bury" to be taken from this source, instead of from the Saxon "byrig," a bridge, when no bridge existed.

Settlements

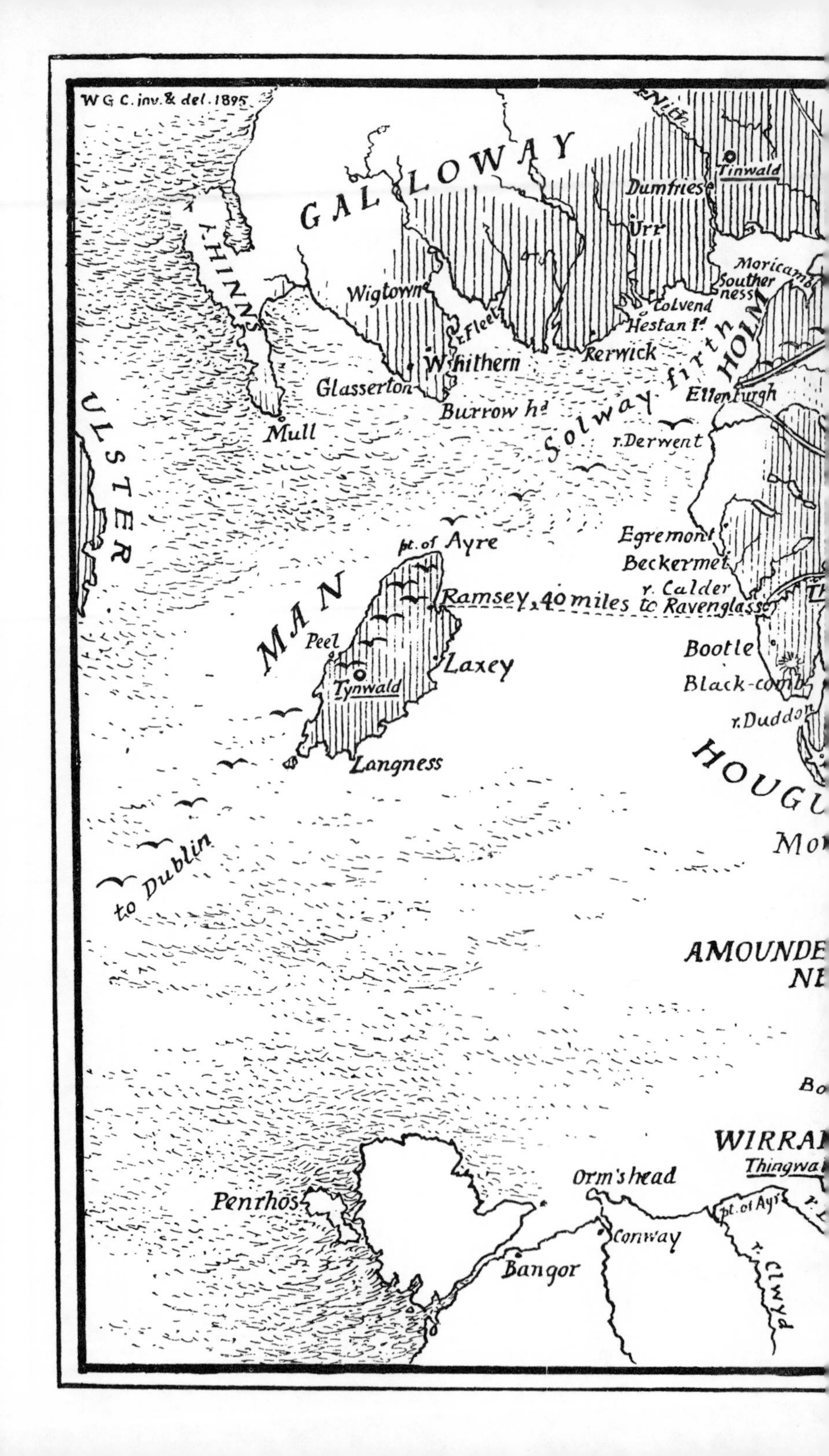
W G C. inv. & del. 1895
GALLOWAY
Nith
Tinwald
Dumfries
Urr
RHINNS
Moricambe
Southerness
Wigtown
Colvend
Hestan Id
r. Fleet
Whithern
Kerwick
Solway firth
HOLM
Glasserton
Ellenburgh
Burrow hd
ULSTER
Mull
r. Derwent
Egremont
pt. of Ayre
Beckermet
r. Calder
MAN
Ramsey, 40 miles to Ravenglass
Peel
Bootle
Laxey
Tynwald
Black-comb
r. Duddon
Langness
HOUGU
Mo
to Dublin
AMOUNDE
NE
Bo
WIRRA
Thingwa
Orm's head
Penrhos
pt. of Ayr
Conway
r. Clwyd
Bangor

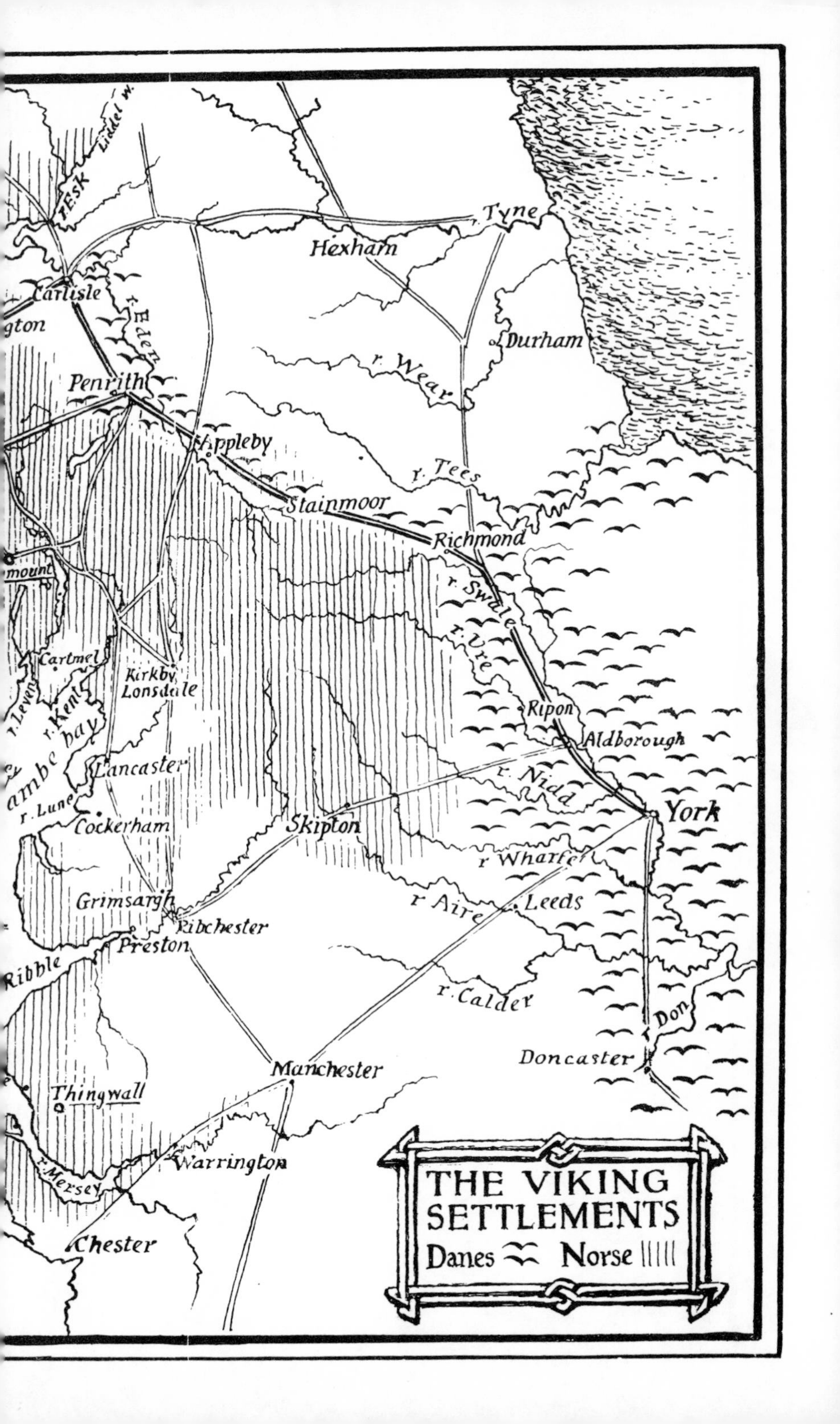

THE VIKING SETTLEMENTS
Danes
Norse
Liddel W.
r. ESK
Carlisle
gton
r. Eden
Penrith
Appleby
Tyne
Hexham
Durham
r. Wear
r. Tees
Stainmoor
Richmond
r. Swale
r. Ure
mount
Cartmel
r. Leven
r. Kent
Kirkby Lonsdale
ambe bay
Lancaster
r. Lune
Cockerham
Ripon
Aldborough
r. Nidd
York
Skipton
r Wharfe
Leeds
r Aire
Grimsargh
Ribchester
Preston
Ribble
r. Calder
Don
Doncaster
Manchester
Thingwall
Warrington
r. Mersey
Chester

CHAPTER II.

Settlements.

From the year 876 the Danes became colonists and settlers. Raid and plunder gave place to peaceful pursuits. The English Chronicle says that in "this year Halfdene apportioned the lands of Northumbria; and they henceforth continued ploughing and tilling them." This colonisation of Deira by the Danes was soon followed in other districts. The greater part of central Britain with the whole of the north and east came entirely under Scandinavian rule.

In 877 trading is recorded by the Sagas from Norway, in a shipload of furs, hides, tallow and dried fish, which were exchanged for wheat, honey, wine and cloth. Thus early was established the increase in comfort and wealth, as evidenced by the erection of Christian monuments early in the tenth century.

The origin of "long-weight" and "long-hundred" count is traceable to the Danish settlements. This peculiar reckoning survives in the selling of cheese 120 lbs. to the cwt., and in the counting of eggs, 120 to the hundred. The timber trade counts 120 deals to the hundred. On the East Coast fish are counted 132 to the hundred.

Six score to the hundred is still popular in Westmorland measure of crops and timber. This Danish method of count was derived from the Icelandic term "hundred" which meant 120.

Professor Maitland, in his "Domesday Book and Beyond," says that the number of sokemen or free men, owing certain dues to the Hundred Court, or to a lord, who were masters of their own land, like the customary tenants of Cumberland, was greater in Norfolk and Suffolk than in Essex, and that in Lincolnshire they formed nearly half the rural population. At the time of Domesday the number of serfs was greatest in the West of England, but none are recorded in Yorkshire and Lincolnshire. In the manors bearing English names the sokemen numbered two-fifths of the population, while in those manors with Danish names they formed three-fifths of the population. (Boyle.)

In the Danelaw they represent the original freeholders of the settlement and owed obedience to the local "Thing" or "Trithing Court." In those districts which were not conquered by Edward the Elder the freeholders settled and prospered, and with the spread of Christianity they became independent proprietors and traders.

The presence of Danish place-names marks the district which they conquered, including the counties of Lincoln, Nottingham, Derby, Leicester, Rutland, and Northampton. In the rest of Mercia few of these names are to be found, viz., in Cheshire,

Shropshire, Staffordshire, Worcester, Gloucester, Hereford and Oxfordshire. The eastern part of the Danish district came to be known as the Five Burghs, namely, Derby, Leicester, Lincoln, Stamford and Nottingham. From the year 880 when Halfdene divided the lands of Deira among his followers the conditions of life became those of colonists, and the Danes settled down to cultivate their own lands, learning the language of the earlier Angles, teaching them many words, and ways of northern handicraft, and gradually intermarrying and forming the vigorous character of body and mind which denotes the modern Englishman.

From the middle of the tenth century men bearing Anglo-Danish names held high positions in the Church; Odo was Archbishop of Canterbury, his nephew Oswald was Bishop of Worcester and afterwards Archbishop of York in succession to Oskytel, and many Norse names appear as witnesses to Royal Charters.

The hatred still existed against these barbarous Danes, and it is recorded in the Saxon Chronicle that the Saxons learned drunkenness from the Danes, a vice from which before they were free. This character is strangely contrasted by the story of John of Wallingford, that "they were wont, after the fashion of their country, to comb their hair every day, to bathe every Saturday, Laugardag, 'bath day,'—and to change their garments often, and to set off their persons by many such frivolous devices.

And in this manner laid siege to the virtue of the women."

If we are to accept the evidence of Lord Coke, we are indebted to the Danish invasion for our propensity to make Ale the national beverage. This eminent authority says that King Edgar, in 'permitting' the Danes to inhabit England, first brought excessive drinking among us.

The word Ale came into the English language through the Danish öl. At any rate after the advent of the Norsemen, the English left off drinking water and began to drink ale as the regular everyday beverage of the people.

The term 'beer' was used by the Anglo-Saxons, but seems to have fallen into desuetude until the name was revived to distinguish 'ale' from hopped ale.'—*From "Inns, Ales, and Drinking Customs of Old England," by Frederick W. Hackwood.*

Green the historian in his "Conquest of England" says the names of the towns and villages of Deira show us in how systematic a way southern Northumbria was parted among its conquerors. . . . "The English population was not displaced, but the lordship of the soil was transferred to the conqueror. The settlers formed a new aristocracy, while the older nobles sank to a lower positon, for throughout Deira the life of an English thane was priced at but half the value of a 'northern hold.'" The inference to be drawn from this passage is that the English lords of the soil were replaced by Danish ones, the English settlers remained in possession of their ancient holdings. In the course of time the two races amalgamated, but at the Norman Conquest this amalgamation had only been partially effected. In the districts where the Danes settled they formed new villages, in which they lived apart from the general Anglian population. Had they not done so the memory of their settlement could never have been perpetuated by the Danish names given to their homes. Every group of isolated Danish place-names teaches the same fact, and there are many such groups. This is the case in the Wirral district of Cheshire, the peninsula between the Mersey and the Dee, where we find such names as Raby, Greasby, Frankby, Irby, Pansby, Whitby and Shotwick, and in the centre of the district the village called Thingwall. While throughout the rest of the county scarcely a Danish name can be found, and as these names were conferred by the Danish settlers it is impossible not to believe that under analogous conditions the names in other districts were conferred in the same way. Where a new village was planted midway between two older villages, its territory would be carved in varying proportions out of the lands of the earlier settlements. Sometimes certain rights of the older villages were maintained in the territory of which they had been deprived. Thus in a Danish village of Anlaby, the lands whereof were carved out of the adjoining townships of Kirk Ella and Hessle, the respective rectors of these parishes had curiously divided rights to both the great and the small tithes; whilst in the neighbouring instance of the Danish Willerby, carved out of Kirk Ella and Cottingham, the rector of Kirk Ella took all the great tithes, and the rector of Cottingham took all the small tithes. This method of Danish *village formation* explains a curious point. The foundation of the earlier Anglian settlements preceded the development of the great road system of England. Leaving out of consideration the Roman roads and the comparatively few British roads, the former of which have relation to nothing but the military needs of that all conquering people, our existing road system is due to the Anglo-Saxon. Our old roads lead from one village to another and each village is a centre from which roads radiate. The Danish villages were, on the contrary, usually roadside settlements. New settlements were formed on the vast fringes of wood and waste which surrounded the cultivated lands of the older English villages. The road existed and the one village street was formed along the line. Such wayside settlements are Carnaby and Bessingby, on the road from Bridlington to Driffield. When, as was sometimes the case, the new settlement was planted at a little distance from the existing road a new road running at right angles from the old one and leading directly to the settlement was formed. Skidby, Towthorp, Kirby, Grindalbythe and many others are cases in point. One consequence of such conditions of formation would be that where the English settlements were most numerous the Danish settlements would be few and small, because there was less land available in such districts for their formation. While, on the other hand, where English settlements were more sparsely scattered the Danish settlements would be more numerous, and comparatively large. Taking a large district like the East Riding, the average area of the Danish townships may be expected to fall below that of the Anglo-Saxon. The facts comply with all these tests.

Thus to take the townships with Danish names, and compare with similar districts of Anglo-Saxon names, we arrive at the conclusion as to whether the district was thickly populated before the coming of the Danes. Many Anglo-Saxon villages are to be found along the course of the Roman road, which coincides with the modern one of to-day. The two classes of population found only in Danish districts, the Sochmanni and the "liber tenentes," are wholly absent in purely English districts. Both held land exempt from villain services, which was a condition of tenure introduced by the Danes. This fact shatters the theory of Green that English settlers were communities of freemen. They were in fact communities of bondmen, villains, bordars, cottars, and serfs, the last holding no lands, but being bound to the soil as chattels, and the rest holding their lands, "at the will of the lord," and in return for actual services. What then was the Sochman? The lawyer of to-day will answer, "He is one who held land by 'socage,' tenure." Although in Domesday this "sochman" is confined to Danish districts, a fact which is recognised in the laws of Edward the Confessor. After the Conquest a type of tenure more or less closely corresponding to that by which the earlier sochman held his land, was gradually established over the whole kingdom.

Tenants who owned such tenures were called "sochmen," and the tenure itself was called "socage." A distinction was drawn between "free socage" and "villain socage." The fuller development of the feudal system which followed the Conquest greatly complicated all questions of land tenure. New conditions of holding superior to that of "socage" were introduced. Thus in the pages of Britton, who always speaks in the person of the King, we read: "Sochmanries are lands and tenements which are not held by knights' fee, nor by grand serjeantries, but by simple services, as lands enfranchised by us, or our predecessors, out of ancient demesnes." Bracton is more explicit. He defines free socage as the tenure of a tenement, whereof the service is rendered in money to the chief lords, and nothing whatever is paid, "ad scutum et servitium regis." "Socage," he proceeds, "is named from soke, and hence the tenants who held in socage are called sochmanni, since they are entirely occupied in agriculture, and of whom wardship and marriage pertain to the nearest parents in the right of blood. And if in any manner homage is taken thereof, as many times is the case, yet the chief lord has not on this account, wardship and marriage, which do not always follow homage." He then goes on to define "villain socage." The essential principle of socage tenure is rent in lieu of services. It is to this fact no doubt that the vast impetus which was given to the coinage of England soon after the coming of the Danes is largely due.

As Mr. Worsaäe says, the Danish coiners increased to fifty in number from the reign of Aethelred to Edward the Confessor, and the greater number exercised this vocation at York and Lincoln. Thus the sochmanni were found only in the settlements of the people who had created in England a tenure of land free from servile obligations.

The manner of fixing these early settlements of land was the same in Ireland, in the East Riding of Yorkshire, and in Lincolnshire. The same custom is still observed by our modern colonists who launch out into the Australian bush. The land was staked out by the settler from the highest ridge downwards to the creek of the river or shore. By this means the settler obtained on outlet to the open sea. The homestead was built by the bondr or husbandman, on the sheltered ground between the marsh and hill. These settlements became byes, and were encircled by a garth, or farmyard. The names of some Norse farms and settlements became composed of a Norse prefix and Saxon ending. Thus we find Oxton "the farm of the yoke," in the hollow of a long ridge. Storeton, from stortun or "big field."

Many of these names are repetitions of places which exist in Cumberland, Denmark, and the Isle of Man. Raby and Irby were smaller farms on the boundary of large byes, and were derived from the Danish chief Ivar. Each homestead had its pastures and woods, which are denoted by the terminals "well," "wall," and "birket," found in such names as Crabwall, Thelwall, Thingwall.

"Thwaites" or "Hlither" were sloping pastures, cleared of wood, between the hill and marsh, used for grazing cattle and sheep. This system of agriculture is of Norse origin, and many such "thwaites" are to be found in Wallasey, Lancashire, and the Lake district. Calday and Calder, recorded in Domesday, "Calders," derived from kalf-gard, are names existing in Calderstones, at Wavertree, and Calday near Windermere, as well as at Eastham and in Scotland. Each large settler had summer pastures for cattle on the highland or moor, called "soeters" or "saetter," a shelter seat for the dairymaids. From this custom we derive the names Seacombe, Satterthwaite, Seathwaite, Seascale, and Sellafield. As the population increased the large estates were divided among the families of the early settlers, and these upland pastures became separate farms. Evidence that these early Norsemen were Christians is found in the name Preston, in Domesday. Prestune, the farm of the priest: who in these early days farmed his own land. From its position this farm became known as West Kirby.

The stone crosses of Nelson and Bromborough prove that these churches were founded early in the eleventh century.

The Danish character of Chester at this date is shown by the fact that it was ruled by "lawmen," in the same manner as the Five Boroughs (vide Round's "Feudal England," p. 465), and its growing wealth and importance was due to the trading intercourse through the Danish ships with Dublin.

Coming from the north-east another Norse and Danish settlement sprang up round Liverpool. Though we have no distinct historical record, the place names indicate the centre was at Thelwall (Tingwall). Such names are Roby, West Derby, Kirkby, Crosby, Formby, Kirkdale, Toxteth, found in Domesday as "Stockestede," Croxteth, Childwall, Harbreck, Ravensmeols, Ormskirk, Altcar, Burscough, Skelmersdale.

Out of forty-five names of places recorded in Domesday in West Derby Hundred, ten are Scandinavian, the rest might be interpreted in either dialect.

All other names in Domesday in South Lancashire are Anglo-Saxon, which only amount to twelve: the reason for the small number of names being that the land was for the most part lying waste, and was thus free from assessment. Thus we find on the present map that Norse names form a large number which are not recorded in Domesday. Many of these would be later settlements. In West Derby the names of three landowners appear in this survey with Norse names, while three others are probably Norse, and seven Saxon.

Following the fall of the Danish dynasty the districts of South Lancashire formed part of Cheshire and we find the names of six "Drengs" around Warrington, possessing Norman names, while only one bears a Norse name. The word "Dreng" being Norse, would infer that the tenure was of "danelaw" origin and not of Anglo-Saxon.

The founder of the Abbey of Burton-on-Trent, Wulfric Spot, held great tracts of land in Wirral and West Lancashire, which are named in his Will dated 1002. Thus the "Bondr" here held his land under Mercian rules, from which the hides and hundreds were similar to those of the previous "danelaw."

Lancashire was the southern portion of Deira, which was one of the two kingdoms, Bernicia being the other, into which the conquests of Ida, king of Northumbria, were on his death divided. In 559 A.D. Ida died, and Aella became King of Deira, and afterwards sole King of Northumbria, until 587 or 589. In 617, Edwin son of Ella was King of Northumbria, the greatest Prince, says Hume the historian, of the Heptarchy in that age. He was slain in battle with Penda of Mercia. In 634 the kingdom was again divided, Eanfrid reigning in Bernicia, and Osric in Deira. Then Oswald, saint as well as king, appears to have reunited the two provinces again under his kingship of Northumberland. Authorities, in more than one instance, vary as to the exact dates, within a year or two.

The Saxon kingdom of Northumbria reached from the Humber to the Forth, and from the North Sea to the Irish Sea. For two centuries after the death of Ecgfrith the Saxon king and the battle of Nectansmere, history only records a succession of plunder and pestilence.

Green the historian says " King after king was swept away by treason and revolt, the country fell into the hands of its turbulent nobles, its very fields lay waste, and the land was scourged by famine and plague."

The pirate Northmen or Vikings as they were called first, began to raid the coast of England with their fleets with the object of plunder. The English Chronicle records their first attacks in the year 787. " Three of their ships landed on the western shores, these were the first ships of Danish men that sought the land of Engle-folk."

The Monastery of Lindisfarne was plundered six years later by their pirate ships, and the coast of Northumbria was ravaged, Jan., 793.

The following year they returned and destroyed the monasteries of Wearmouth and Jarrow. This was the beginning of the Norse raids on our Eastern shores.

In 875 Halfdan returned from his campaign against Alfred and the year after he divided the lands of Northumbria amongst his followers. In many parts we find groups of Scandinavian place-names so close and thick, says Mr. W. G. Collingwood in his "Scandinavian Britain," that we must assume either depopulation by war, or the nearly complete absence of previous population.

There is no reason to suppose that the earlier Vikings depopulated the country they ravaged. Spoil was their object and slaughter an incident,

As Canon Atkinson has shown in his "Analysis of the Area of Cleveland under Cultivation at Domesday Period," very little of the country in that district was other than moor or forest at the end of the eleventh century, and that most of the villages then existing had Scandinavian names. His conclusion is that these districts were a wilderness since Roman and prehistoric days, and first penetrated by the Danes and Norse: except for some clearings such as Crathorne, Stokesley, Stainton, and Easington, and the old monastery at Whitby.

This conclusion receives support, says Mr. Collingwood, from an analysis of the sculptured stones now to be seen in the old Churches and sites of Cleveland. It is only at Yarm, Crathorne, Stainton, Easington, and Whitby, that we find monuments of the pre-Viking age, and these are the products of the latest Anglian period.

At Osmotherley, Ingleby, Arncliffe, Welbury, Kirklevington, Thornaby, Ormesby. Skelton, Great Ayton, Kirkdale, and Kirkby-in-Cleveland are tombstones of the tenth and eleventh centuries. It is thus evident that the Angles were only beginning to penetrate these northern parts of Yorkshire when the Vikings invaded and carried on the work of land settlement much further. Further extension was made by the Norse from the West Coast, as the place-names show. Monuments of pre-Viking art work exist at places with Scandinavian names, such as Kirkby-Moorside, Kirkby-Misperton, and Kirkdale; while in other cases only Viking age Crosses are found at places with names of Anglian origin, such as Ellerburn, Levisham, Sinnington, Nunnington.

This would indicate that some Anglian sites were depopulated and refounded with Danish names, while others had no importance in Anglian times but soon became flourishing sites under the Danes.

In the west of Yorkshire the great dales were already tenanted by the Angles, but the moors between them, and the sites higher up the valleys, were not the sites of Churches until the Danish period. (See " Anglian and Anglo-Danish Sculpture in the North Riding," by W. G. Collingwood. *Yorks. Arch. Journal*, 1907.)

Yorkshire at the time of the Domesday survey was carucated and divided into Ridings and Wapentakes. Thingwall, near Whitby. (Canon Atkinson, site lost.) Thinghow, near Ginsborough (now lost), and Thinghow, now Finney Hill, near Northallerton. (Mr. William Brown, F.S.A.) Tingley, near Wakefield; Thingwall, near Liverpool; Thingwall in Wirral, may have been Thingsteads. (W. G. Collingwood.)

Names of places ending in -ergh, and -ark are dairy-farms from setr and saetr. Names with ulls- as prefix, such as Ulpha, Ullscarth, Ullswater, record the fact that wolves inhabited the hills.

Beacons were kept up in olden days on hills which bear the names of Warton, Warcop, Warwick and Warthole. Tanshelf, near Pontefract, is derived from Taddenesscylfe, Blawith and Blowick from Blakogr—blackwood. Axle, Acle, arcle from öxl, the shoulder.

The Battle of Brunanburh.

Was it Fought in Lancashire?

"There is one entry in the Anglo-Saxon Chronicle which must be mentioned here as it throws light upon an archæological discovery of considerable importance. In 911 the Chronicle records that the Danish army among the Northumbrians broke the peace and overran the land of Mercia. When the King learned that they were gone out to plunder, he sent his forces after them, both of the West Saxons and the Mercians; and they fought against them and put them to flight, and slew many thousands of them. . . ."

"There is good reason to believe," as Mr. Andrew shows (Brit. Numis. Jour. i, 9), "that the famous Cuerdale hoard of Silver coins, which was found in 1840 in a leaden chest buried near a difficult ford of the Ribble on the river bank about two miles above Preston, represents the treasure chest of this Danish army, overtaken in its retreat to Northumbria at this ford and destroyed."

Then follows a process of reasoning in support of the above conclusion, based upon the place of minting and the dating of the coins.

"The bulk of the coins, however, were Danish, issued by Danish Kings of Northumbria, many of them from York."

Besides the Cuerdale find of 10,000 silver coins and 1,000 ounces of silver there are records given of other Danish finds.—From the Victoria County History of Lancashire, Vol. I., see Coins.

Each historian of this important event has claimed a different site, in as many parts of England. In Grose's "Antiquities" we find the allied Scotch, Welsh, Irish, and Danes, the Northumbrian army, under Anlaf were totally defeated, in 938 at Brunanburgh (Bromridge, Brinkburn), in Northumberland, when Constantine, King of the Scots, and six petty Princes of Ireland and Wales, with twelve Earls were slain. This description is given in the Anglo-Saxon Chronicle. The honour of claiming the Lancashire site on the river Brun near Burnley, belongs to the late Mr. Thomas Turner Wilkinson, a master of Burnley Grammar School, who claimed it for Saxifield in 1856.

We are indebted to Mr. Jas. T. Marquis, a member of the Lancashire and Cheshire Antiquarian Society, for the following summary of evidence which he placed before the above Society during the winter session of 1908-9, and which will be found recorded in the Transactions of the Society. He says, "There is overwhelming testimony in favour of the site on the Lancashire Brun."

The reasons for claiming this site are simply two. An old writer spells Brinkburn—Brincaburh, and there is an artificial mound proving a fight.

Camden gives Brunford, near Brumbridge in Northumberland, as the place where "King Athelstane fought a pitched battle against the Danes." This might easily be, but not the battle we refer to. There is no reason given except the word "ford."

Gibson suggests that it must have been "somewhere near the Humber," although he finds a difficulty in carrying Constantine and the little King of Cumberland so high into Yorkshire. The other places suggested are Brumborough in Cheshire, Banbury in Oxfordshire, Burnham and Bourne in Lincolnshire, Brunton in Northumberland, but no good reason beyond a name, and an embankment in some cases, but not all. Brownedge in Lancashire has been suggested, with excellent reasons.

Dr. Giles and others suggest that the name should be Brumby instead of Brunanburh. Ingram in his map of Saxon England places the site in Lincolnshire, near the Trent, but without assigning good reasons. Turner observes that the "Villare" mentions a Brunton in Northumberland, and Gibson states what may still be seen in maps of a century old, "that in Cheshire there is a place called Brunburh near the shores of the Mersey." This last would be a serious competitor if there was a river Brun, or tumuli, or ford, or battlefield: but nothing is claimed, only the name suggested.

Brunsford or Brunford. Let us first establish the site of the "burh," which is a hill that shields or protects a camp, town, or hamlet. The question is, where was the "tun" or village on the Brun? It was in Saxon times usual for the folk to settle near a "burh" for the protection afforded by an overlord who occupied it.

It was also the custom of the early missionaries to establish a feldekirk by setting up a Cross near to the hamlet, where they used to preach Christianity and bury their dead.

Tradition says it was intended to build the Church on the site of the Cross, but that God willed it otherwise. God-ley Lane would be the lane which led from the village in Saxon times to God's Lea or God-ley, on which was the new church and burial ground. Thus the new town would take its modern name from the ground on which the Church stood, namely Brun-ley, Bron-ley, and Burn-ley.

The cross, built in Saxon times to mark the spot where Christianity was first preached, stood at the foot of the "burh" near the Brun, and thus the early name would be Brunford.

The records of Domesday Book contain no mention of Burnley. To the east and west would be the vast forest of Boulsworth and Pendle, while the valleys would be marshes and swamps. The ancient roads went along the hill sides, and there is an ancient road from Clitheroe by Pendle passing along the east side of the hill, now almost obliterated, leading to Barrowford. The ancient road on this east side of the valley, was on the Boulsworth slope from Brunford, via Haggate and Shelfield, to Castercliffe, Colne, and Trawden which gave its name to the forest, and Emmott.

Dr. Whitaker tells us that in his day, "in the fields about Red Lees are many strange inequalities in the ground, something like obscure appearances of foundations, or perhaps entrenchments, which the levelling operations of agriculture have not been able to efface. Below Walshaw is a dyke stretching across from 'Scrogg Wood' to 'Dark Wood.'"

The ninth century annalist says, "The Northmen protected themselves according to custom, 'with wood and a heap of earth.'" A Walshaw would therefore be a wall of wood. Nothing was safer, when attacked by bowmen, than a wood. Such was the Brun-burh. This burh at Red Lees with mounds and ditches, in a half circle on each side of the Causeway, would have the same appearance on being approached from the east and south-east as the eleventh century "burh" at Laughton-en-le-Morthen in Yorkshire.

The ancient way referred to in Dr. Whitaker, from Burnley to Townley, would be from the Market Cross, along Godley Lane to the Brunford Cross, up over the ridge to the top of Brunshaw, along the Causeway to Lodge Farm, through the Deer Park, through the Watch Gate at the foot of the hill, and up to Castle Hill at Tunlay.

Although Egbert was called the first King of England, his son Alfred the Great at the height of his power only signed himself "Alfred of the West Saxons, King."

England was still governed under the three provinces at the time of Henry I., namely Wessex, Mercia, and Danelagh. The latter province comprised the whole tract of country north and east of Watling Street. Mercia included the lands north of the Mersey. Danish Northumbria or Deira comprised the lands to the west of the Pennines.

Amongst the hills north of the Ribble the hostile nations could meet in security. Saxon-Mercia north of the Mersey, surrounded by alien nations, and having been itself conquered from that claimed as the Danelaw, would be the most likely where those nations could meet in time of peace, and was the debatable land in time of war.

After the death of Alfred, when Edward the Elder claimed overlordship, the Danes rose in revolt in the north. It is recorded that he and his warrior sister "the Lady of the Mercians" abandoned the older strategy of rapine and raid, for that of siege and fortress building, or the making and strengthening of burhs.

Edward seems to have recovered the land between the Mersey and the Ribble, for soon after leaving Manchester, the Britons of Strathclyde, the King of Scots, Regnold of Bamborough who had taken York at this period, and the Danish Northumbrians take him to be father and lord. The place is not mentioned, but must be somewhere between Boulsworth and Pendle.

The same thing happened when Athelstan claimed his overlordship. Profiting by following his father's example, he would travel from burh to burh, and his route would not be difficult to trace, namely, Thelwall, Manchester, Bacup, Broad Dyke, Long Dyke, Easden Fort, Copy Nook, Castle Hill,

Extwistle Hall, near Eamott, marks an ancient boundary.

Watch Gate, Brunburh, Broadbank, Castercliffe, Shelfield, Winewall, Eamot.

The Anglo-Saxon Chronicle says that "A.D. 926, Sihtric perished, and King Athelstan ruled all the Kings in the Island, the Northumbrians, Constantine King of Scots, Ealdred of Bamborough, and others, which they confirmed by pledges and oaths at a place Eamot on the 4th of the ides of July and they renounced idolatry."

Everything points to the fact that Brunanburgh gave its name to this battle. This part of the Saxon king's dominions being the one place where all the hostile nations could meet before the attack.

There is no other river Brun in northern Mercia, and the Saxon Chronicle says the battle was fought near Brunanburh.

Ethelward says Brunandune (river and dale). Simeon gives Wendune (Swindon). Malmesbury and Tugulf names Brunanburh or Bruford. Florence of Worcester "near Brunanburh." Henry of Huntingdon gives Brunesburh, and Gaimar has Brunswerc, which we have in Worsthorne, which is known to be derived from Wrthston, the town of Wrth. In the *Annales Cambriae* it is styled the "Bellum Brun" (the Battles of the Brun). This would explain the many names.

William of Malmesbury says that the field was "far into England." We have Brownedge and Brownside. In addition to all this we have "Bishops Leap," S'Winless Lane, Saxifield, Saxifield Dyke. We have also a Ruh-ley, a Red Lees, directly opposite to which we have a traditional battlefield and battlestone, also a High Law Hill, and Horelaw Pastures, a number of cairns of stones, a small tumuli; all of which may be said to be near the hillfort Brunburh.

Descriptions of Battles from the Map.

From the two Ordnance maps, "six inch to the mile," one of Briercliffe, and the other of Worsthorne, it may be seen that the roads from Slack, near Huddersfield, pass through the Pennine range, one by the long Causeway, on the south of the position and on the southern side, near Stipernden, is "Warcock Hill. From here running north, are a series of ridges, Shedden Edge, Hazel Edge, Hamilton Hill, to the other road from Slack, passing through the hills at Widdop, and immediately on the north side at Thursden is another Warcock Hill. From Warcock Hill to Warcock Hill would stretch the army of Anlaf in their first position. From the north end of the position a road north to Shelfield and Castercliffe, by means of which he would be joined by his Welsh allies, from the Ribble, via Portfield, and his Strathclyde and Cumbrian allies from the north. From this end of the position there is a road due west to the Broadbank, where there is the site of a small camp at Haggate.

From here Anlaf would send his Welsh allies

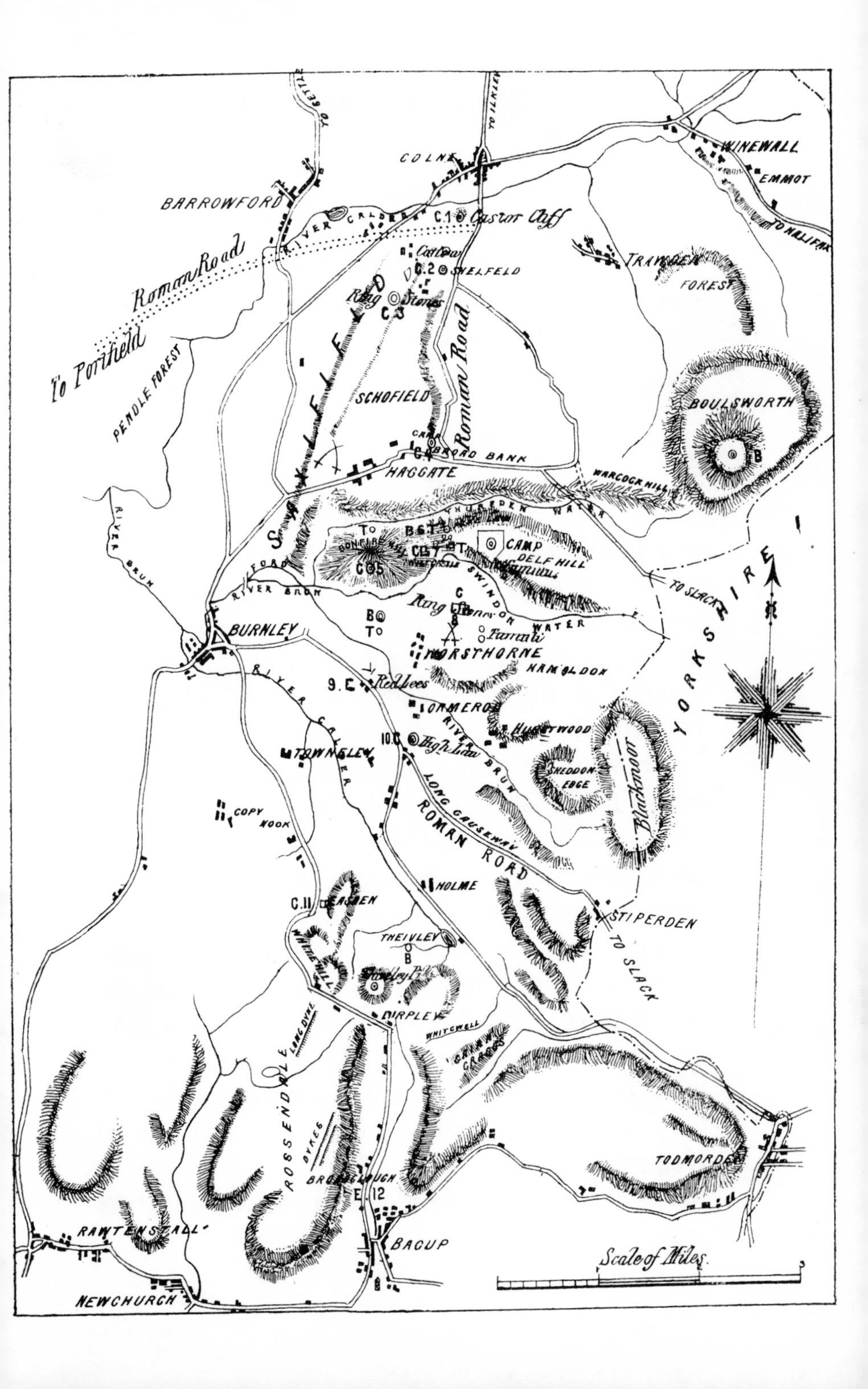

TO SETTLE
TO ILKLEY
COLNE
WINEWALL
EMMOT
BARROWFORD
RIVER CALDER
C.1 Castor Cliff
TO HALIFAX
Roman Road
C.2 SHELFELD
TRAWDEN
FOREST
Ring Stones
C.3
To Porthfield
PENDLE FOREST
Roman Road
SCHOFIELD
BOULSWORTH
B
BROAD BANK
HAGGATE
WARCOCK HILL
THURSDEN WATER
RIVER BRUN
CAMP
DELF HILL
BONFIRE HILL
C.O.5
FORD
SWINDON
RIVER BRUN
TO SLACK
YORKSHIRE
Ring Stones
SWINDON WATER
BURNLEY
WORSTHORNE
HAMELDON
9.E
Red Lees
RIVER CALDER
ORMEROD
RIVER BRUN
HURSTWOOD
10.C
High Law
TOWNELEY
SHEDDON EDGE
Blackmoor
LONG CAUSEWAY
ROMAN ROAD
COPY NOOK
HOLME
C.11
STIPERDEN
TO SLACK
B
DIRPLEY
WHITEWELL
LONG DYKE
ROSSENDALE
DYKES
TODMORDEN
E.12
RAWTENSTALL
BACUP
Scale of Miles
NEWCHURCH

under Adalis, and his shipmen under Hryngri, for the night attack on the advancing Saxons as they crossed the Brunford. They fell on them somewhere on the site of Bishop's House Estate, but were afterwards beaten back across the estates known as Saxifield. Two days afterwards both sides prepared for the great struggle near the burh, and Anlaf, taking his cue from his opponent, advanced his left and took possession of the hill near Mereclough, afterwards called High Law (Round Hill), and the pastures behind still known as Battlefield, with a stone called Battlestone in the centre of it.

Constantine and the Scots were in charge of the hill, and the Pict, and Orkney men behind. His centre he pushed forward at Brown Edge, to the "Tun of Wrst." While his right touched S'Winden Water under Adalis with the Welsh and shipmen.

Two days before the great battle Athelstan marched out of Brunburh at the north end, and encamped somewhere on the plain called Bishop's House Estate, his route by the Brunford, and probably S'Winless Lane.

We are told that Anlaf entered the camp as a spy, and ascertaining the position of Athelstan's tent, formed the night attack for the purpose of destroying him. Athelstan, however, leaving for another part of his position on the Brun, gave Wersthan, Bishop of Sherborne, the command.

The Bishop met his death somewhere on the estate, the Pasture being known as Bishop's Leap, which undoubtedly gave its name to the estate.

Adalis, the Welsh Prince, had done this in the night attack, probably coming by way of Walshaw, and Darkwood. Alfgier took up the command, with Thorolf on his right and Eglis in support in front of the wood. Alfgier was first assaulted by Adalis with the Welsh and driven off the field, afterwards fleeing the country. Thorolf was assaulted by Hryngr the Dane, and soon afterwards by Adalis also, flushed with victory. Thorolf directed his colleague Eglis to assist him, exhorted by his troops to stand close, and if overpowered to retreat to the wood. Thorolf or Thorold the Viking was the hero of this day, near the Netherwood on Thursden Water. He fought his way to Hryngr's standard and slew him. His success animated his followers, and Adalis, mourning the death of Hryngr, gave way and retreated, with his followers back over Saxifield to the Causeway camp at Broadbank.

Whatever took place at Saxifield the enemy left it entirely, and the decisive battle took place at the other end of Brunburh. In walking up S'Windene, by S'Winden Water, the district on the right between that river and the Brun is called in old maps Roo-ley and in older manuscripts Ruhlie, marked in Thomas Turner Wilkinson's time, with a cairn and tumulus. Some distance further on we find Heckenhurst. The roads down from the burh are at Rooley and at Brownside and at Red Lees by the Long Causeway leading to Mereclough.

Athelstan placed Thorolf on the left of his army, at Roo-ley, to oppose the Welsh and irregular Irish under Adalis. In front of Brownside (Burnside) was Eglis with the picked troops, and on Eglis' right opposite Worsthorne, Athelstane and his Anglo-Saxons.

Across the original Long Causeway on the Red Lees, with the burh entrenchments immediately at his back, was the valiant Turketul, the Chancellor, with the warriors of Mercia and London opposite Round Hill and Mereclough.

Thorolf began by trying to turn the enemy's right flank, but Adalis darted out from behind the wood, now Hackenhurst, and destroyed Thorolf, and his foremost friends on Roo-ley or Ruhlie. Eglis came up to assist his brother Viking, and encouraging the retreating troops by an effort destroyed the Welsh Prince Adalis, and drove his troops out of the wood. The memorial of this flight was a cairn and tumulus on Roo-ley.

Athelstan and Anlaf were fighting in the centre for the possession of (Bruns) Weston, neither making much progress, when the Chancellor Turketul, with picked men, including the Worcester men under the magnanimous Sinfin, made a flank attack at Mereclough, and breaking through the defence of the Pict and Orkney men, got to the

"Back o' th' Hill." He penetrated to the Cumbrians and Scots, under Constantine, King of the Grampians. The fight was all round Constantine's son, who was unhorsed. The Chancellor was nearly lost, and the Prince released, when Sinfin, with a mighty effort, terminated the fight by slaying the Prince.

On Round Hill, down to one hundred years ago, stood a cairn called High Law. When the stones were made use of to mend the roads, a skeleton was found underneath. That would, I believe, be a memorial of the fight.

At "Back o' th' Hill," a blind road leads through what in an old map, and in tradition is called "Battlefield," and the first memorial stone is called "Battlestone." Another similar stone is further on. Following the blind road through Hurstwood, the Chancellor would find himself at Brown End, near Brown Edge. At the other end of the position, Eglis having won the wood, would be in the neighbourhood of Hell Clough, ready to charge at the same time as Turketul, on the rear of Anlaf's army.

At this point of the battle, Athelstan, seeing this, made a successful effort and pushed back the centre. Then began the carnage, the memorials of which are still to be seen on Brown Edge, Hamilton Pasture, Swindene, Twist Hill, Bonfire Hill, and even beyond. Those who could get through the hills at Widdop would do so: others however would take their "hoards" from the camps at

Old Daneshouse

Warcock Hill and other places, and burying their "treasures" as they went along, pass in front of Boulsworth, and over the moor through Trawden Forest, between Emmott and Wycollar.

If the Saxon description of the battle, in Turner's "History of the Anglo-Saxons" be read and compared with the Ordnance maps before named, the reader will see that there is no other place in England which can show the same circumstantial evidence nor any place, having that evidence, be other than the place sought for.

Danes House, Burnley, is thus referred to by the late Mr. T. T. Wilkinson, F.R.A.S.:—"Danes House is now a deserted mansion situated about half-a-mile to the north of Burnley, on the Colne Road. It has been conjectured there was a residence on the same site A.D. 937, when Athelstan, King of the South Saxons, overthrew with great slaughter, at the famous battle of Brunanburgh, Anlaf, the Dane, and Constantine, King of the Scots. Tradition states that it was here that Anlaf rested on his way to the battlefield from Dublin and the Isles, hence the name Danes House. The present deserted mansion has undergone little change since it was re-erected about the year 1500." This house has now been pulled down.

The Dyke or Dykes, Broadclough, Bacup.

This mighty entrenchment is over 600 yards in length and for over 400 yards of the line is 18 yards broad at the bottom. No satisfactory solution has yet been offered of the cause of this gigantic work or of the use to which it was put originally. Speaking of it Newbigging (" History of Rossendale ") says :—

" The careful investigations of Mr. Wilkinson have invested this singular work with more of interest than had before been associated with it, by his having with marked ability and perseverance, collected together a mass of exhaustive evidence, enforced by a chain of argument the most conclusive, with regard to the much debated locality of the great struggle between the Saxons and the Danes, which he endeavours, and most successfully, to show is to be found in the immediate neighbourhood of Burnley, and in connection with which the earthwork in question constituted, probably, a not unimportant adjunct."

Again, he says :—

" If Saxonfield (Saxifield) near Burnley, was the scene of the engagement between the troops of Athelstan and Anlaf, then it is in the highest degree probable that one or other of the rival armies, most likely that of the Saxon King, forced, or attempted to force a passage through the valley of the Irwell and that there they were encountered by the confederated hosts intrenched behind the vast earthwork at Broadclough that commanded the line of their march. Whether this was taken in flank or rear by the Saxon warriors, or whether it was successful in arresting their progress, or delaying a portion of their army, it is impossible to determine; but that it was constructed for weighty strategical purposes, under the belief that its position was of the last importance, so much of the remains of the extraordinary which still exists affords sufficient evidence."

Place - Names

CHAPTER III.

Place-Names.

An eloquent modern writer has declared, with a good reason, that even if all other records had perished, "anyone with skill to analyse the language, might re-create for himself the history of the people speaking that language, and might come to appreciate the divers elements out of which that people was composed, in what proportion they were mingled, and in what succession they followed one upon the other." From a careful analysis of the names of the more prominent features of the land; of its divisions, its towns and villages, and even its streets, as well as the nomenclature of its legal, civil, and political institutions, its implements of agriculture, its weapons of war, and its articles of food and clothing,—all these will yield a vast fund of history.

The place-name Liverpool has been the greatest puzzle to local etymologists. From the earliest known spelling—recorded in a deed of the time of Richard I. 1189-99, where the form is Leverpool—to the present, it has gone through more changes than any other local name. As the Norse element in the vicinity of Liverpool has been very great, we may assume the original derivation to come from "hlith," the old Norse for a "slope." The north dialect also contains the word "lither" meaning sluggish. It is an adjective bearing the same meaning as the modern English "lithe," pliant, or gentle. The names Lithgoe, Lethbridge, Clitheroe, and Litherland may be derived from it.

From the peaceful reign of Canute, or Knut, we derive the nautical term, some place-names—Knuts-ford, Knott End, Knot Mill, Knottingley. Knot, from old Norse "Knutr," and "Knotta," a ball, was the name given to the measurement of speed of a ship. Fifty feet was the distance allowed between the knots on the cord, and as many as ran out in half a minute by the sand-glass indicated the speed of the ship. And thus we speak of a 10 knot breeze blowing.*

Hope, as a place-name, is common from the Orkneys to the Midlands, and is derived from an old Norse word "hoop," for a small land-locked bay, inlet or a small enclosed valley, or branch from the main dale. Hope is a common place-name, as well as a surname. In compounds we find it in Hopekirk, Hopeton, Hapton, Hopehead, Dryhope.

From "Trow," a trough, we derive Trowbridge, Troughton, Trawden, and probably Rawtenstall.

The battle of Brunanburg, which took place in the year 937, is supposed to have been fought on the site of the modern Burnley, on the river Brun. King

* Knott is also used for the name of a mountain or hill, as in Arnside Knott, in Westmoreland, but near the Lancashire border.

Olaf brought his men over in 600 ships, many containing over 100 men each. He was defeated by Athelstane and his brother Edmund. There was until recently pulled down in Burnley a house called Danes-house. Though the Danes lost this battle, the northern bards recorded its bravery in their war songs, of which their Sagas or legends still preserve some remains.

Among the chief followers of King Athelstane in 931, who subdued the Danish kingdom in England, we find the names of the following Jarls: Urm, Gudrum, Ingrard, Hadder, Haward, Healden, Rengwald, Scule, and Gunner. It is not difficult to recognise modern surnames from this list, such as Urmston, Guthrie, Hodder, Howard, Holden, Heald, Reynolds, Scholes, and Gunning.

"Northumbria was the literary centre of the Christian world in Western Europe," says John Richard Green; and the learning of the age was directed by the Northumbrian scholar Baeda, the venerable Bede.

Yorkshire.

The population of Yorkshire, after the retreat of the Romans, was composed of Angles.

When the Vikings invaded the county, the wide dales only had been occupied by these early settlers. The higher valleys were densely wooded, the broad moors and mosslands had not been penetrated until the coming of the Norse in 900 A.D.

Some Anglian districts were refounded under Danish names, and became flourishing settlements. Canon Atkinson has shown by his analysis of Cleveland, that at Domesday, very little of that district was under cultivation. To the end of the eleventh century it consisted of moor and forest, and that many of the villages had then Danish names. The name Ingleby shows the passing of the Angles, by the addition of the Danish 'by.'

At Domesday Yorkshire was divided into Ridings (thrithings), and Wapentakes.

Such names as Thingwall near Whitby, Thinghow near Gainsborough, Thinghow near Northallerton, and Tingley near Wakefield, though some of the sites have disappeared, remain to show the centres of Danish government. The presence of many Scandinavian places and names suggests that the country before then was a wilderness. The condition of the country may be gathered from the records and traditions of Reginald and Symeon of Durham. In 875 Halfdan the Dane began his raid into Bernicia, and the Abbot of Lindisfarne, Eardwulf fled before him, taking the relics of St. Cuthbert. These wanderings, says Symeon, covered a period of nine years. The leader of this band was Eadred, the Abbot of Carlisle (Caer-Luel), whose monastery had been destroyed, and with the city, lay in ruins for two hundred years. At the places where these relics rested during their wanderings, Churches were afterwards erected, and dedicated to this Saint. The direction taken by the fugitives has been traced by Monsignor Eyre and the late Rev. T. Lees, first inland to Elsdon, then by the Reed and Tyne to Haydon Bridge, and up the Tyne valley; south by the Maiden way, and then through the fells by Lorton and Embleton to the Cumberland coast. At Derwentmouth, Workington, they determined to embark for Ireland, but were driven back by a storm and thrown ashore on the coast of Galloway, where they found a refuge at Whithorn.

Mr. W. G. Collingwood says in his "Scandinavian Britain," that in this storm the MS. Gospels of Bishop Eadfirth (now in the British Museum) were washed overboard, but recovered. At Whithorn the bishop heard of Halfdan's death, and turned homewards by way of Kirkcudbright.

The fact that the relics of St. Cuthbert found refuge in Cumberland and Galloway shows that the Danish invasion, from which they were saved, took very little hold of these parts. The Vikings of the Irish Sea were already under the influence of Christians, if not christianised, and were not hostile to the fugitive monks, while the natives welcomed them.

The early historians relate the curious story of the election of Guthred, Halfdan's successor. Eadred, Abbot of Carlisle, who was with St. Cuthbert's relics at Craik, in central Yorkshire, on the way home, dreamt that St. Cuthbert told him to go to the Danish army on the Tyne, and to ransom from slavery, a boy named Guthred, son of Hardecnut (John of Wallingford says, "the sons of Hardecnut had sold him into slavery"), and to present him to the army as their king. He was also to ask the army to give him the land between the Tyne and the Wear, as a gift to St. Cuthbert and a sanctuary for criminals. Confident in his mission, he carried out its directions; found the boy, ransomed him, gained the army's consent, and the gift of the land, and proclaimed Guthred King at "Oswigedune." Eardwulf then brought to the same place the relics of St. Cuthbert, on which every one swore good faith. The relics remained until 999 at Chester-le-Street, and there Eardwulf re-established the bishopric.

In these records of the Saxon historian Symeon, we have the curious illustration of the Viking raiders becoming rapidly transformed from enemies into allies and rulers chosen from among them. The history of Guthred's reign was peaceful, and he became a Christian King. His election took place about the year 880. During the reign of Guthred, his kingdom became christianised, the sees of Lindisfarne and York survived the changes. Guthred died in 894 and was buried in the high church at York.

In 919 Ragnvald, called by Symeon "Inguald," became King of York. He was one of the most romantic figures of the whole Viking history. His name bore many forms of spelling: Ragnvald, Reignold, Ronald, Ranald, and Reginald.

Coming from the family of Ivar in Ireland, Ragnvald mac Bicloch ravaged Scotland in 912, fought and killed Bard Ottarsson in 914 off the Isle of Man. Joined his brother at Waterford in 915 and set out for his adventure in North Britain. Landing in Cumberland, he passed along the Roman wall, and becoming King of York, was the first of the Irish Vikings who ruled until 954.

The attacks of Vikings who were still Pagans continued, and many curious lights are shed by the chronicles of Pictish writers. The power of St. Cuthbert over the lands given for a sanctuary to Eadred the Abbot, is recorded in the legend of Olaf Ball (from 'ballr,' the stubborn), a Pagan who refused rent and service to St. Cuthbert, for lands granted to him by Ragnvald, between Castle Eden and the Wear. This Pagan came one day to the Church of St. Cuthbert at Chester-le-Street. He shouted to Bishop Cutheard and his congregation, "What can your dead man, Cuthbert, do to me? What is the use of threatening me with his anger? I swear by my strong gods, Thor and Uthan, that I will be the enemy of you all from this time forth." Then, when he tried to leave the Church, he could not lift his foot over the threshold, but fell down dead. "And St. Cuthbert, as was just, thus got his lands."

The succession of races which gave many of our

place-names, and the order in which they came, has been pointed out in the following names by the late Canon Hume, of Liverpool: Maeshir, now called Mackerfield, was called Maeshir by the Britons, meaning longfield; to which the Saxons added field, which now becomes Longfield-field, Wansbeckwater is Danish, Saxon, and English, three words meaning water. Then we have Torpenhowhill, a hill in Cumberland, composed of four words, each meaning hill.

In addition to maritime terms, and terms of government, we derive from Danish sources titles of honour and dignity, such as king, queen, earl, knight, and sheriff.

The Danes have left us traces of their occupation in the word gate, which is of frequent occurrence, and used instead of street in many of our older towns. The Saxons, who were less civilised, left many terms, such as ton, ham, stead, and stock. But they had no word to denote a line of houses. "Gata" was therefore not the English word used for gate, but a street of houses. From the Norman we have row, from rue, a street.

The names of many of our streets and buildings are full of historical associations and information. In Bolton, Wigan, and Preston we find some streets bearing the name of gate, such as Bradshawgate, Wallgate, Standishgate, and Fishergate. In the towns of York, Ripon, Newcastle, and Carlisle many more of these gates are to be found. York has no less than twenty gates.

To the roads of the Romans, the Danes gave the name of "a braut," *i.e.*, the broken course, or cleared way. (From this "a braut" comes the modern English word abroad, and the adjective broad.) The Anglo-Saxon took the name of street from the Roman strata. Thus we get the name of Broad Street, being two words of similar meaning.

Lone, lonely, and alone come from "i laun," which means banishment, and those thus outlawed formed the brigands of the hill districts. We thus get Lunesdale, Lune, and Lancaster, from which John of Gaunt took his English title.

Skipper was the Danish term for the master of a small vessel. In the game of bowls and curling the skipper is the leader or director.

"Hay," the Norse for headland, pronounced hoy, furnishes us with several local place-names, such as Huyton, Hoylake, Howick.

A Norse Festival.

Trafalgar Day is celebrated by the usual custom on October 21st—by the hoisting of the British flag on the public buildings and by the decoration of the Nelson Monuments in Liverpool and London. This battle was fought in 1805, and decided the supremacy of Britain as a sea power. Long may the deathless signal of our greatest hero continue to be the lode star of the man and the nation: "England expects that every man will do his duty."

Let us trace the connection between Lord Nelson and the Danes in our own county. Admiral Nelson bore a genuine Scandinavian name, from "Nielsen," and was a native of one of the districts which were early colonised by the Danes, namely, Burnham-thorpe, in Norfolk. His family were connected with the village of Mawdesley, near Rufford, which still has for its chief industry basket-making. Fairhurst Hall, at Parbold, in the same district of Lancashire, was the home of a Nelson family for many centuries.

This recalls the fact that we have still in existence a curious survival. "A strange festival" is celebrated each year on January 31st at Lerwick, or Kirkwall, the capital of the Orkney Isles. The festival called "Up-helly-a" seems to be growing in favour. Lerwick becomes the Mecca of the North for many days, and young people travel long distances to witness the revels that go to make up the celebration of the ancient festival. All former occasions were eclipsed by the last display. At half-past eight o'clock a crowd of about 3,000 people assembled in the square at the Market Cross. In the centre stood a Norse war galley or Viking ship, with its huge dragon head towering upwards with graceful bend. Along the bulwarks were hung the warriors' shields in glowing colours, the Norse flag, with the raven, floating overhead. On board the galley fiddlers were seated. Then a light flared below Fort Charlotte, which announced that the good ship Victory would soon be on the scene. And a stately ship she was, as she came majestically along, hauled by a squad in sailor costume, while a troop of instructors from the Fort walked alongside as a guard of honour to the good vessel. The Victory immediately took up her position, and the guizers began to gather. Torches were served out, the bugle sounded the call to light up, and then the procession started on its way round the town. The guizers who took part numbered over three hundred, and seen under the glare of the torches the procession was one of the prettiest. The Norse galley led the way, and the Victory occupied a place near the centre of the procession. The dresses were very tasteful and represented every age and clime. There were gay Cavaliers, Red Indians, Knight Templars, and squires of the Georgian period. The procession being over, the Victory and the Norse galley were drawn up alongside each other, near the market cross, while the guizers formed a circle round them. Toasts were proposed, songs were sung, and thereafter the proceedings were brought to a close by the guizers throwing their flaming torches on board the ships. As soon as the bonfire was thoroughly ablaze, the guizers formed themselves in their various squads, each headed by a fiddler, and began their house to house visitation. The guizer was costumed as an old Norse jarl, with a sparkling coat of mail, and carried a prettily emblazoned shield and sword. The squad of which he was chief were got up as Vikings. Curiously enough, these were followed by Dutch vrows.

The Orkneys and Shetland Isles were ceded to James III. of Scotland, as the dowry of his wife, Margaret, in 1469, and became part of Great Britain on the union of Scotland with England. James I. married Ann of Denmark, and passed through Lancashire in August, 1617, when he visited Hoghton Tower. The effusiveness of the Prestonians was outdone at Hoghton Tower, where His Majesty received a private address in which he was apostrophised as "Dread Lord." He is reported to have exclaimed "Cot's splutters! What a set of liegemen Jamie has!"

Patronymics

CHAPTER IV.

Patronymics.

We are sprung from the sea; a county of seaports is our dwelling-place, and the sea itself our ample dominion, covered throughout its vast extent with our fellow subjects in their "floating cities." These are filled with our wealth, which we commit to the winds and waves to distribute to the extremities of the four quarters of the world. We are therefore no common people, nor are they common events which form eras in our history; nor common revolutions which have combined and modified the elements of our speech.

Though we have kept no genealogies to record to us from what particular horde of settlers we are sprung—no family chronicles to tell us whether Saxon, Dane, Norse, or Norman owns us as progeny—still our names serve partly to distinguish us, and "words" themselves thus still remind us of what otherwise would be totally forgotten. It has been claimed that two-thirds of us are sprung from the Anglo-Saxons and Danes, and had our language kept pace with our blood we should have had about two-thirds of our modern English of the same origin. But we have more. Our tongue is, hence, less mixed than our blood. It is therefore easier to trace out the histories of words than of families.

It is difficult at first sight to determine whether family names have been derived from family residences or the residences have obtained their names from their first proprietors. The Romans imposed their military names upon the towns of the early Britons. The Danes added their own descrip-names, and previous to becoming converted to Christianity gave the names of their heathen deities to the mountains and landmarks. To these were added the names of Norse and Danish kings and jarls. After the Norman Conquest, when the land had been divided by William the Conqueror among his followers, comes the period when surnames were taken from the chief lands and residences. Pagan deities supply us with many surnames. From "Balder" comes Balderstone, Osbaldistone. "Thor" gives us Tursdale, Turton, Thursby, Thorley, Thurston, and Thurstaston, in the Wirral, near West Kirby. "Frëyer" supplies Frisby, Frankby, Fry, Fryer, Fraisthorpe, and Fraser. "Uller" or "Oller" gives Elswick, Ullersthorpe, Elston, Ulverston. From "Vé," a sacred place, like "Viborg," the old Jutland assize town, we derive Wydale, Wigthorpe, Wythorpe, Willoughby, Wilbeforce, Wigton, and Wyre. Some of our earliest Lancashire names are derived from "Gorm," "Billingr," "Rollo," who were Norse and Danish kings. Their names and their compounds show us that the Danes were Christianised, as "Ormskirk," which provides very many surnames, such as Orme, Oram, Ormsby, Ormerod, Ormeshaw; and another form of Gorm, "Grim" as Grimshaw and Grimsargh. Formby and Hornby may also be traced to this origin. From "Billingr" we get Billinge, the village near Wigan, standing on a high hill and having a beacon, Billington and other names of this construction. From "Rollo" we derive Roby, Raby, Rollo, Rollinson, Ribby. From "Arving," an heir, we get Irving, Irvin, and Irton. From "Oter" we have Otter, Ottley, Uttley. The Danes sailed up the river Douglas, and gave the name Tarleton, from "Jarlstown." Many Christian names come from the Danish—Eric, Elsie, Karl, Harold, Hugo, Magnus, Olave, Ralph, Ronald, Reginald. Surnames formed by the addition of "son" or "sen" are common to both Danes and English, but never appear in Saxon names. Thus we have Anderson, Adamson, Howson, Haldan, Matheson, Nelson, Jackson, Johnson, Thomson, and Stevenson.

The different names we find given to the same trees arise from different settlers giving and using their own form of name: "Birch," "Bracken," "Crabtree," and "Cawthorn." "Wil-ding" is also known in Westmorland and Yorkshire. "Whasset," which gives its name to a small hamlet near Beetham, in Westmorland, is Danish; "Wil-ding" is probably Flemish, and also Wild, Wilde, as this name dates from about the year A.D. 1338, when Eward III. encouraged numbers of Flemings to come over from the Netherlands to introduce and improve the manufacture of woollens. He located them in different parts of the country, and we find them settled in Kendal and in the vicinity of Bury and Rochdale. This will account for this surname being so frequently found in Lancashire.

From Copenhagen "the harbour of merchants," we derive many important place-names and surnames. A Copeman was a Chapman, a merchant or dealer; and thus we derive Cheap, Cheapside, Chepstow, and Chipping. In surnames we get Copeland, Copley, Copethorne, and Capenhurst. The common expression "to chop or change," comes from this source. In the London Lyckpeny of 1430 we find: "Flemings began on me for to cry 'Master, what will you copen or buy.'" In 1579, Calvin in a sermon said: "They play the copemaisters, and make merchandise of the doctrine of this Gospel." These early copmen remind us of the Lancashire merchant who had visited the States after the American Civil War. He said to the late John Bright: "How I should like to return here, fifty years after my death, to see what wonderful progress these people have made." John Bright replied: "I have no doubt, sir, you will be glad of any excuse to come back."

To the abundance of surnames derived from

Danish origin the following are important:—Lund, Lindsey, Lyster, Galt or Geld, and Kell. Lund was a grove where pagan rites were conducted. Lindsey is a grove by the sea. Lyster is Danish for a fishing fork composed of barbed iron spikes on a pole for spearing fish. Galt or Geld, an offering of the expiatory barrow pig to the god "Frëyer." From Kell, in Danish a "spring," we get Kellet and Okell.

Surnames of a distinct Danish character, and customs derived from Viking days are to be met with in our local Fairs and Wakes. Writing on this subject, the Rev. W. T. Bulpit of Southport says that, "Robert de Cowdray, who died in 1222, was an enterprising Lord of Manor of Meols, and obtained a Charter from the King, with whom he was a *Persona-Grata*, for a weekly Wednesday market, and a yearly Fair, to be held on the Eve and Day of St Cuthbert, to whom the church is dedicated.

The Charter probably did but legalise what already existed; Cowdray was a man of the world, and knew that it would be an advantage to his estate to have a fair.

Soon after his death the Charter lapsed. Enemies said it interfered with pre-existing fairs.

Though legally it had no existence the fair continued for centuries in connection with St. Cuthbert's wake in March. It was also the end of the civil year, when payments had to be made, and thus farm stock was sold. This caused the market and wake to be useful adjuncts, and a preparation for welcoming the New Year on March 25th, St Cuthbert's Day, the anniversary of his death was held on March 23rd, and a Viking custom demanded a feast. The old name of the death feast was called Darval, and the name was transferred to the cakes eaten at the wake, and they were called Darvel Cakes.*

Long after the event commemorated was forgotten Darvel Cakes were supplied in Lent to guests at Churchtown wakes.

Connected with these fairs there was a ceremony of electing officials, and at these social gatherings of all the local celebrities a Mayor was elected who generally distinguished himself by being hospitable. Similar ceremonies still exist, where charters no longer survive, at such places as Poulton near Blackpool, and Norden near Rochdale.

Traces of the Norman are found in Dunham Massey and Darcy Lever and a few others, but along the whole of the east and north of the county the Saxon and Danish landholder seems to have held in peace the ancestral manor house in which he had dwelt before the Conquest, and the haughty insolence of the Norman was comparatively unknown. Speke, the oldest manor house in South Lancashire, near Liverpool, is derived from "Spika," Norse for mast, which was used for fattening swine. "Parr" is a wooded hill, and this word enters into many compound names. "Bold,"

* From Darvel—death and öl—feast.

near St. Helens, signifies a stone house, and is the surname of one of the oldest Lancashire families. The Norse "Brecka," a gentle declivity, is much in evidence in West Lancashire, as in Norbreck, Warbrick, Swarbrick, Torbrick, Killbrick in the Fylde district, and also Scarisbrick, in the vicinity of Ormskirk. This name used to be spelt Scaursbreck, and is a compound of "Scaur," a bird of the seagull type, and "breck" from the natural formation of the land. Birkdale, Ainsdale, Skelmersdale, Kirkdale, Ansdell, Kirby, Kirkby, Crosby, are all place-names of Danish origin which provide many surnames in the county. Where Danish names abound the dialect still partakes of a Danish character.

English Surnames.

A great majority are derived from trades and callings. Some may be traced from ancient words which have dropped out. "Chaucer"* and "Sutor" are now meaningless, but long ago both signified a shoemaker. A "pilcher" formerly made greatcoats; a "Reader," thatched buildings with reeds or straw; a "Latimer" was a writer in Latin for legal and such like purposes. An "Arkwright" was the maker of the great meal chests or "arks," which were formerly essential pieces of household furniture; "Tucker" was a fuller; "Lorimer" was

* The ancestors of the poet were, however, more likely "Chaussiers," makers of long hose.

a sadler; "Launder" or "Lavender," a washerman; "Tupper" made tubs; "Jenner" was a joiner; "Barker" a tanner; "Dexter," a charwoman; "Bannister" kept a bath; "Sanger" is a corruption of singer or minstrel; "Bowcher," a butcher; "Milner" a miller; "Forster," a forester; a "Chapman" was a merchant. The ancestors of the Colemans and Woodyers sold those commodities in former generations; "Wagners" were waggoners; and "Naylors" made nails. A "Kemp" was once a term for a soldier; a "Vavasour" held rank between a knight and a baron. Certain old-fashioned Christian names or quaint corruptions of them have given rise to patronymics which at first sight appear hard to interpret. Everyone is not aware that Austin is identical with Augustin; and the name Anstice is but the shortening of Anastasius. Ellis was originally derived from Elias. Hood in like manner is but a modern corruption of the ancient Odo, or Odin. Everett is not far removed from the once not uncommon Christian name Everard, while even Stiggins can be safely referred to the northern hero "Stigand." The termination "ing," signified son or "offspring." Thus Browning and Whiting in this way would mean the dark or fair children. A number of ancient words for rural objects have long ago become obsolete. "Cowdray" in olden days signified a grove of hazel; "Garnett," a granary. The suffix "Bec" in Ashbec and Holmbec is a survival of the Danish "by," a habitation. "Dean" signifies a hollow or dell, and the word "bottom" meant the same thing. Thus Higginbottom meant a dell where the "hicken" or mountain ash flourished. "Beckett" is a little brook, from the Norse "beck." "Boys" is a corruption of "bois," the French for wood. "Donne" means a down; "Holt," a grove, and "Hurst," a copse. "Brock" was the old term for a badger, hence Broxbourne; while "Gos" in Gosford signified a goose.

On Dialect in Lancashire and Yorkshire.

The district of England which during the Heptarchy was, and since has been known by the name of Northumbria, which consists of the territory lying to the north of the rivers Humber (whence the name North-humbria) and Mersey, which form the southern boundaries, and extending north as far as the rivers Tweed and Forth, is generally known to vary considerably in the speech of its inhabitants from the rest of England. Considering the great extent and importance of this district, comprising as it does more than one-fourth of the area and population of England, it seems surprising that the attention of philologists should not have been more drawn to the fact of this difference and its causes. From an essay on some of the leading characteristics of the dialects spoken in the six northern counties of England (ancient Northumbria) by the late Robert Backhouse Peacock, edited by the Rev. T. C.

Atkinson, 1869, we learn that, when addressing themselves to the subject of dialect, investigators have essayed to examine it through the medium of its written rather than its spoken language. The characteristics to be found in the language now spoken have been preserved in a degree of purity which does not appertain to the English of the present day. It is therefore from the dialect rather than from any literary monuments that we must obtain the evidence necessary for ascertaining the extent to which this Northumbrian differs from English in its grammatical forms,—not to speak of its general vocabulary.

The most remarkable characteristic is the definite article, or the demonstrative pronoun—"t," which is an abbreviation of the old Norse neuter demonstrative pronoun "hit"—Swedish and Danish "et." That this abbreviation is not simply an elision of the letters "he" from the English article "*the*," which is of old Frisian origin, is apparent from the fact that all the versions of the second chapter, verse 1, for instance, of Solomon's Song, "I am the rose of Sharon, and the lily of the valleys," the uniform abbreviation for all parts of England is the elision of the final letter "e," making *the* into "th"; on the other hand, out of fourteen specimens of the same verse in Northumbria, eight give the "t" occurring three times in the verse, thus, "I's t' rooaz o' Sharon, an' t' lily o' t' valleys."

The districts where the Scandinavian article so

abbreviated prevails are found in the versions to be the county of Durham, Central and South Cumberland, Westmorland; all Lancashire, except the South-eastern district, and all Yorkshire; an area which comprehends on the map about three-fourths of all Northumbria.

The next leading feature is the proposition—i, which is used for in. This is also a pure Scandinavianism, being not only old Norse, but used in Icelandic, Swedish and Danish of the present day. Two instances occur in the 14th verse of the same chapter, where for "O my dove, thou art in the clefts of the rock, in the secret places of the stairs, etc.," we have idiomatic version: "O my cushat, 'at 's i' t' grikes o' t' crags, i' t' darkin' whols o' t' stairs."

Another word which occurs in six of the Northumbrian versions is also Scandinavian, viz., the relative pronoun *at* for *that*. From this illustration of a short verse and a half of Scripture, we have established the Norse character of the dialect as distinguished from common English, of five of the most ordinary words in the English language, namely, the representatives of the words *the*, *in*, *that*, *art* and *am*. These instances from the Etymology of the Dialects help to establish the following canon: That when a provincial word is common to more than one dialect district (that is, districts where in other respects the dialects differ from each other), it may, as a rule, be relied upon, that the word is not a corruption but a legitimate inheritance. Those referred to, we have seen, are the inheritance of a whole province, that province being formerly an entire kingdom.

Proceeding in the usual order of grammars, having disposed of the article, we come next to the *substantives.* These differ from the ordinary English in that they recognise only one "case" where English has two. The Northumbrian dialect dispenses with the possessive or genitive case almost entirely, and for "my father's hat," or "my uncle's wife's mother's house," say, "my faddher hat," and "my uncle wife muddher house." Upon which, all that need be remarked is that they have gone further in simplifying this part of speech than the rest of their countrymen, who have only abolished the dative and accusative cases from the parent languages of their speech. Extreme brevity and simplicity are eminently Norse and Northumbrian characteristics. We have already seen some remarkable instances in the versions of Solomon's Song, where we saw that the first three words, "I am the," are expressed in as many letters, namely, "I's t'; and again in verse 14, "thou art in the," by "at 's i t'." We have here another instance in the abolition of the genitive case-ending, out of many more that might be added.

In pronouncing the days of the week we find: Sunnda for Sunday, Thorsda for Thursday, and Setterda for Saturday, always with the short da. The remaining days as in ordinary English.

In pronouns we find "wer" for "our," in the possessive case, from old Norse vârr.

Relative—*At* for who, which, that.
Demonstrative—T' The.
That theyar—that one.
Thoer—these or those.

Indefinites—Summat=something, somewhat. From old Norse sum-hvat, somewhat.

The two following are common at Preston and adjacent districts:

Sooawhaasse=whosoever.
Sooawheddersa=whethersoever.

Correlative adjectival pronoun:
Sa mich=so much.
Swedish, Sâ mycket.

Adverbs from Scandinavian:
Backerds—backwards.
Connily—prettily, nicely.
eigh—yes; forrùt, forrud—forwards;
helder—preferably: i mornin—to-morrow;
i now—presently; lang sen—long since;
lowsley—loosely; neddher—lower nether;
neya—no; noo—now;
reetly—rightly; sa—so; sen—since;
Shamfully—Shamefully.
Shaply—shapely; sooa—so.
tull—to; weel—well; whaar—where.

Interjections.

Ech!—exclamation of delight.

Hoity-toity!—what's the matter: from old Norse "hutututu."

Woe-werth!—woe betide.

AN ILLUSTRATION.

A good illustration of Danish terms may be gathered from the following conversation heard by a minister in this county between a poor man on his death-bed and a farmer's wife, who had come to visit him: "Well, John," she said, "when yo' getten theer yo'll may happen see eaur Tummus; and yo'll tell 'im we'n had th' shandry mended, un a new pig-stoye built, un 'at we dun pretty well beawt him." "Beli' me, Meary!" he answered, "dost think at aw's nowt for t' do bo go clumpin' up un deawn t' skoies a seechin' yo're Tummus!" The word "mun" also is in frequent use, and comes from the Danish verb "monne;" the Danish "swiga," to drink in, as "to tak a good swig," and "Heaw he swigged at it!" Many Danish words become purely English, as foul, fowl; kow, cow; fued, food; stued, stood; drown, drown; "forenoun" and "atternoun" became "forenoon" and "afternoon;" stalker, stalker; kok, cock; want, to want.

In popular superstition the races had much in common. The Danish river sprite "Nok," imagined by some to be "Nick," or "Owd Nick," the devil; but properly "Nix," a "brownie." He wore a red cap and teased the peasants who tried to "flit" (Danish "flytter") in order to escape him.

Though we have "Gretan," to weep, it also means to salute or bid farewell, from the Danish "grata." "Give o'er greeting," we hear it said to a crying child. While "greeting" is a popular word of Danish origin, so is "Yuletide" for Christmas, and "Yule Candles," "Yule Cakes," "Yule Log." The word "Tandle" means fire or light, and is given to a hill near Oldham. From this we derive our "Candle." "Lake," to play, is still used in our district, but never heard where Danish words are not prevalent. In the Danish, "Slat" means to slop, and it is said, "He slat the water up and down." A very common participle in Lancashire is "beawn." The Danish "buinn" is "prepared," or "addressed to," or "bound for," as "Weere ar't beawn furt' goo?" In Danish and Lancashire "ling" means heath; but it does not occur in Anglo-Saxon. From the Danish "Snig," to creep, we get "snig," eels.

Locally we also have the name "Rossendale," which covers a large extent of our county. May we not suppose this to be from "rost," a torrent or whirlpool, and "dale," the Danish for valley?

The names of places beginning or ending with "Garth," or "Gaard," shows that the people were settling in "Gaarde" or farms belonging to the chief, earl, or Udaller. With the Danish "Steen," for stone, we have Garston, Garstang, Garton, as well as Garswood and garden.

The Danish having no such sound or dipthong as our 'th," must account for the relic of the pronunciation "at" for "that," which is much used in our local dialect, as "It's toime at he were here,"—"at" being the Danish conjunction for "that." The word we use for sprinkling water, to "deg," does not come from the Anglo-Saxon "deagan," which means to dye or tinge with colour, but from "deog" or "deigr." Shakespeare uses the word in the "Tempest," where Prospero says: "When I have deck'd the sea with drops full salt." From "Klumbr," a mass or clod, we get "clump," as clump of wood, and "clumpin' clogs." Stowe says, "He brought his wooden shoes or clumpers with him."

Physical Types Still Existing

CHAPTER V.

PHYSICAL TYPES STILL EXISTING.

As early as the eleventh century the names of English towns and villages are written in the Domesday Book with the Danish ending " by " or " bi," and not with the Norwegian form of " böer " or " bö." This preponderance of Danish endings proves the widely extended influence of the Danes in the North. That they should have been preserved in such numbers for more than eight centures after the fall of the Danish dominion in England, disproves the opinion that the old Danish inhabitants of the country were supplanted or expelled after the cessation of the Danish rule (1042), first by the Anglo-Saxons, and afterwards by the Normans. Mr. Wörsæ says: " The Danes must have continued to reside in great numbers in these districts, previously conquered by them, and consequently it follows that a considerable part of the present population may with certainty trace their origin to the Northmen, and especially to the Danes. The general appearance of the inhabitants is a weighty corroboration of the assertions of history. The black hair, dark eye, the prominent nose, and the long oval face to be found in the Southerners remind us of the relationship with the Romans, or a strong mixture of the British Anglo-Saxon and Norman races. The difference in physiognomy and stature of the Northern races are also easily be recognised. The form of face is broader, the cheekbones stand out prominently, the nose is flatter, and at times turned somewhat upwards. The eyes and hair are of a lighter colour, and even deep red hair is far from uncommon. The people are not very tall in stature, but usually more compact and strongly built than those of the South."

The still existing popular dialect is an excellent proof that the resemblance of the inhabitants is not confined to an accidental or personal likeness. Many words and phrases are preserved in the local dialect which are neither found nor understood in other parts of the country. These terms are not only given to waterfalls, mountains, rivulets, fords, and islands, but are also in common use in daily life. The housewife has her spool and spinning wheel from "spole"; her reel and yarn-winder from "rock" and "granwindle"; her baking-board from "bagebord." She is about to knead dough, from "deig"; and in order to make oaten bread, or thin cakes beaten out by the hand, we have clap-bread or clap-cake, form "klapperbröd" and "klapper-kake." She spreads the tablecloth, "bordclaith," for dinner, "onden"; while the fire smokes, "reeks," as it makes its way through the thatch, "thack," where in olden times the loft, "loft," was the upper

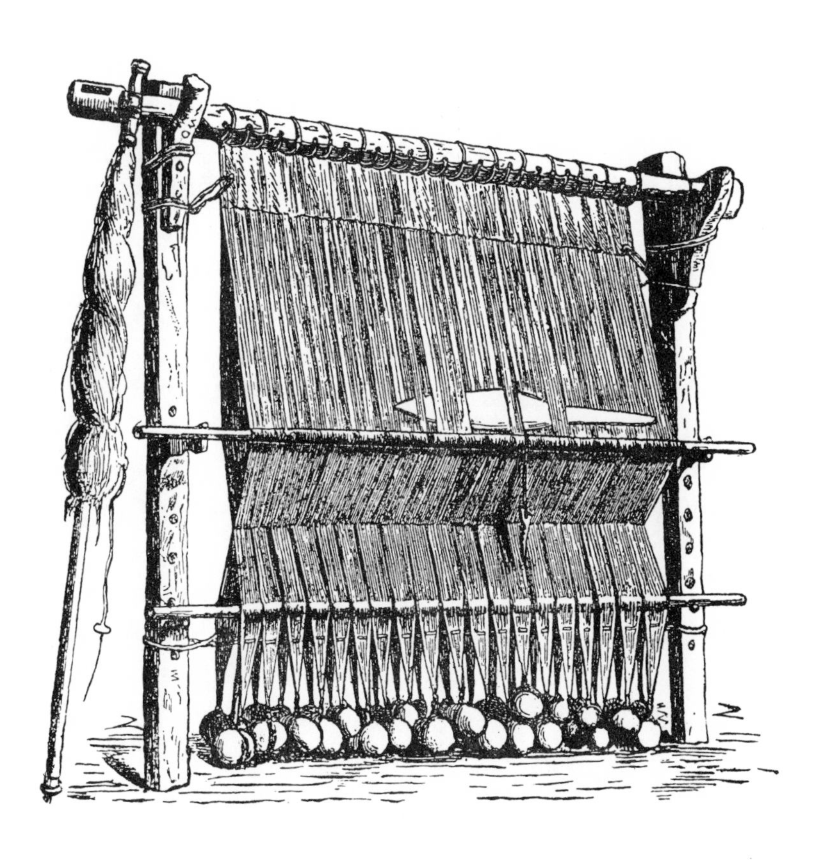

Example of Ancient Danish Loom ; from the Färoes, now in Bergen Museum.

room or bower, "buir." Out in the yard or "gaard," is the barn, "lade," where is stored the corn in "threaves." In the river are troughs, "trows," used to cross over. These were two small boats, cut out of the trunks of trees, and held together by a cross-pole. By placing a foot in each trough the shepherd rowed himself across with the help of an oar. He goes up the valley, "updaal," to clip, "klippe," the sheep. It is said that Canute the Great crossed over the river Severn in this manner, when he concluded an agreement with Edmund Ironsides to divide England between them. Blether, from "Bladdra," is also a common expression, meaning to "blubber or cry," to gabble or talk without purpose. Another form of the word is "bleat," as applied to sheep.

Other words now in use from the Norse are "twinter," a two-year-old sheep, and "trinter," a three-year-old. A "gimmer lamb" is a female lamb. The lug-mark, *i.e.*, a bit cut out of a sheep's ear that it may be recognised by the owner, is from lögg mark." Lög is law, and thus it is the legal mark. The "smit" or smear of colour, generally red, by which the sheep are marked occurs in the Bible of Ulphilas in the same sense as smear. Another proof may be found on the carving in the knitting sticks made and used by the Northern peasantry of the present day. The patterns are decidedly Scandinavian.

Of the people of this district, it may be said that

in their physical attributes they are the finest race in the British dominions. Their Scandinavian descent, their constant exposure to a highly oxygenised atmosphere, their hereditary passion for athletic sports and exercises, their happy temperament, their exemption from privation, and many other causes, have contributed to develop and maintain their physical pre-eminence, and to enable them to enjoy as pastime an amount of exposure and fatigue that few but they would willingly encounter. Thomas de Quincey, who lived thirty years among them, observed them very closely, and knew them, well, after remarking that "it is the lower classes that in every nation form the 'fundus' in which lies the national face, as well as the national character," says: "Each exists here in racy purity and integrity, not disturbed by alien inter-marriages, nor in the other by novelties of opinion, or other casual effects derived from education and reading." The same author says: "There you saw old men whose heads would have been studies for Guido; there you saw the most colossal and stately figures among the young men that England has to show; there the most beautiful young women. There it was that sometimes I saw a lovelier face than ever I shall see again." The eloquent opium-eater gave the strongest possible proof that his admiration was real by taking one of these "beautiful young women" to wife.

The men of our northern dales do not pay much

respect to anyone who addresses them in language they are not accustomed to, nor do they make much allowance for ignorance of their own dialect. In a northern village we once stopped to speak to an old lady at her door, and began by remarking that the river was much swollen. "We call it a beck," said the old lady, turning her back upon us, and telling her granddaughter to bring out the scrapple. "Whatever may a scrapple be?" we asked, deferentially. "Why, that's what a scrapple may be," she said, indicating a coal-rake in the girl's hand. As we moved away, we overheard her say to a neighbour, "I don't know where he has been brought up. He calls th' beck a river, and doesn't know what a scrapple is!" They have a very quick sense of humour, and often practice a little mystification on inquisitive strangers. To a tourist who made the somewhat stupid inquiry, "Does it ever rain here?" the countrymen replied: "Why it donks, and it dozzles, and sometimes gives a bit of a snifter, but it ne'er comes in any girt pell," leaving the querist's stock of information very much as he found it.

The first invasion of the Danes took place in the year 787, and to Scotland they gave the name of "Sutherland," and the Hebrides were the southern islands, or "Sudreygar," a name which survives in the title of the Bishop of Sodor and Man.

The Forest of Rossendale contains eleven "vaccaries," or cow-pastures (we are told by Mr. H. C. March, M.D.), which were called "booths," from the huts of the shepherds and cowherds. From this we trace Cowpebooth, Bacopbooth, and Crawshawbooth. Booth is derived from the old Norse "bûd," a dwelling, while from "byr" and "boer" we get the surnames Byrom, Burton, Buerton, Bamber, Thornber. "Forseti" was the judge of one of the Norse deities, and the word supplies us with Fawcett, Facit, or Facid as it was spelt in 1781, and Foster. Unal was a Danish chief, whose name survives as a surname Neal, Niel, and O'Neil. From the old Norse "yarborg," an earthwork, we get Yarborough, Yerburgh, Sedburg, and Sedberg. Boundaries have always been matters of great importance, and "twistle" is a boundary betwixt farms. Endrod was King of Norway in 784, and his name furnishes Endr, whose boundary becomes Entwistle, and also Enderby. Rochdale is derived from "rockr," old Norse for rock, and dale from the Norse "daal," a wide valley; thus the Norsename Rochdale supplanted Celtic-Saxon name of "Rachdam." "Gamul," meaning old, was a common personal name among Norsemen. In a grant of land dated 1051, fifteen years before the Conquest, appears the name of Gouse Gamelson, which is a distinct Norse patronymic. Gambleside was one of the vaccaries or cow-pastures of Rossendale Forest, and was spelt Gambulside. In Anglo-Saxon and Teutonic dialects "ing" is a patronymic, as in Bruning, son of Brun, says Mr. Robert Ferguson, M.P., in his "Surnames as a Science." But it has also a wider sense. Thus, in Leamington it signifies the people of the Leam, on which river the place is situated. From a like origin comes the name of the Scandinavian Vikings, Vik-ing; the people from Vik, a bay. Sir J. Picton, in his "Ethnology of Wiltshire," says: "When the Saxons first invaded England they came in tribes, and families headed by their patriarchal leaders. Each tribe was called by its leader's name, with the termination 'ing,' signifying family. Where they settled they gave their patriarchal name to the mark, or central point round which they clustered."

Considering the great number of these names, amounting to over a thousand in England, and the manner in which they are dispersed, it is impossible to consider them as anything else than the everyday names of men. This large number will serve to give an idea of the very great extent to which place-names are formed from the names of men who founded the settlements. It must be remembered that the earlier date now generally assigned for the Teutonic settlements tends to give greater latitude to the inquiry as to the races by whom the settlements were made, as well as the fact that all our settlements were made in heathen times. From the neighbouring tribe of Picts we retain one form "pecthun," from which we derive the surnames of Picton, Peyton, and Paton. This may suggest that we owe the name peat to the same origin. We have also the word pictures, probably formed from "pict," and "heri," a warrior.

Political Freemen

CHAPTER VI.

Political Freemen

Under the reign of Ethelred II. the supremacy of the Anglo-Saxons had already passed away. As a people they sank, and left only a part of their civilisation and institutions to their successors, the Danes and Normans. The development of a maritime skill unknown before, of a bold manly spirit of enterprise, and of a political liberty which, by preserving a balance between the freedom of the nobles and of the rest of the people, ensured to England a powerful and peaceful existence.

Danish settlers in England conferred a great benefit on the country, from a political point of view, by the introduction of a numerous class of independent peasantry. These people formed a striking contrast to the oppressed race of Anglo-Saxons. Turner says: "The Danes seem to have planted in the colonies they occupied a numerous race of freemen, and their counties seem to have been well peopled." The number of these independent landowners was consequently greatest in the districts which were earliest occupied by the Danes, where they naturally sprung up from the Danish chiefs parcelling out the soil to their victorious warriors.

Twenty years after the Norman Conquest there was a greater number of independent landed proprietors, if not, in the strictest sense of the word, freeholders, in the districts occupied by the Danes, and under "Danelag," than in any other of the Anglo-Saxon parts of England. The smaller Anglo-Saxon agriculturists were frequently serfs, while the Danish settlers, being conquerors, were mostly freemen, and in general proprietors of the soil.

Domesday Book mentions, under the name of "Sochmanni," a numerous class of landowners or peasants in the Danish districts of the north, while in the south they are rarely to be found. They were not freeholders in the present sense of the term. They stood in a feudal relation to a superior lord, but in such a manner that the "Sochmanni" may best be compared with our present "hereditary lessees." Their farm passed by inheritance to their sons, they paying certain rents and performing certain feudal duties; but the feudal lord had no power to dispose of the property as he pleased.

The following is an abstract of a paper on Tithe and Tenure in the North, by the Rev. J. H. Colligan:—

Danish Influence on Land Tenure

was originally a military one. In Westmorland the manors were granted round several great baronies or Fees. The barons held their estates "in capite" from the king, upon conditions that were mainly military, while the lords of the manors held of the barons, their chief duty being, to keep a muster-roll of their tenants for the discharge of the military claims of the barons. The tenants held of the lord by fines and services, the latter being, until the close of the XVIth century, of a military character. This baronial system, perfected by William the Conqueror, gave enormous power into the hands of the barons.

The Hudlestons, of Millum Castle, Lancashire, exercised the prerogative of "jura regalia" for twenty-two generations. They also had the privileges of "wreck of the sea." Some of the barons had the power of capital punishment, others, again, had the right to nominate sheriffs. They held their own courts and could be either friends or rivals of the king, to whom alone they owed homage, with service at home or abroad. The authority thus obtained by the barons was distributed to the knights and lords of the manors, who, in their turn, levied conditions upon their dependants.

This system of devolution of power received from the king was enjoyed also by the church, and kept the counties always ready for war. When the martial spirit began to forsake the land, and peaceful and sporting pleasures arose, we find a new form of tenure. Lands and tenements are given for the apparently trifling conditions of keeping up eyries of hawks for the baron, or of providing a gilt spur, or of producing a rose, sometimes out of season but generally in the time of roses, or of making presents of pepper, ginger, cloves, or some other tasty trifle. A number of these rents require no explanation, as they are only the reflex of the passion of the age. Horses, dogs and hawks for the knight, pepper, ginger and cloves for the monks, are easily understood. The reasons for the rose and stirrup, the spur and the glove are not so apparent. It is possible that originally they were symbolical of real rent or service. The transition from the actual to the symbolical must have taken place in the XIVth and XVth centuries.

We have hitherto been speaking of the relationship between the barons and the monks, the knights and the lords of the manor. There is no reference to tenants, because there was no such thing as a free individual tenure before the middle of the XVIth century. The soldier-tenants clung round the barony of the manor, and their position was defined as "tenantes ad voluntatem." It was only in Elizabeth's reign that the demands of the tenants began to be formulated, and the unique form of tenure called "tenant right" appeared on the border. It is difficult to discover when and how the movement for freedom on the part of the tenants began, but it certainly is associated with the Reformation, and is seen plainly in those places where protestantism was vigorous.

We shall examine the growth of this form of tenure as it appeared in a Cumberland manor. In the neighbourhood under consideration we find three kinds of tenants. At the one extreme were the Drenges, who were probably Saxon slaves; at the other were tenants by right, who were probably equal in dignity and privilege in the early days to the lord of the manor himself. In Cumberland and Westmoreland traces of the Drengage tenements may be found, and the Bondgate, Appleby, is an illustration of Drengage dwellings. The tenants by right are found in Cumberland, where they are now called yeomen, and in Westmorland, where they are known as statesmen (steadsmen), and in North Lancashire, where, to the regret of the writer in the Victoria County History, the yeomen are gradually disappearing. Mr. J. Brownbill says that tenant right was frequently urged all over Furness and Cartmel and in Warton and the northern border of Lancashire. He refers to the particulars in West's "Antiquities of Furness."

We have not been able to ascertain the origin of the tenure as it applies to North Lancashire, but on the borders it is the outcome of an interesting and unique form of service called Cornage. It is still a disputed point as to the origin of the word. Some holding it to from the fact that the lord gave notice of the enemies' approach by winding a horn; others that it was much earlier in its origin, and arises from the horn or cattle tax, still known in Westmorland as neat- or nowt-geld. Whichever origin be taken, it is clear that, from the time of Queen Elizabeth, the keeping of the borders was an important service, and is seen from the fact that the tenant could not hire another to take his place.

In regard to this border service, known as Cornage, the lord had several privileges which included wardship or control over the heir, until he was 21 years of age; marriage, which gave him the right of arranging a marriage if the inheritance had devolved upon a female; and relief, which was the payment of a certain sum by the heir upon taking possession of the inheritance. The chief privilege which the "tenant-by-right" possessed for his border service was that of devising his tenement by *will*, a privilege which is much prized until this day. At the Restoration the "Drengage tenure" was raised into a Socage tenure, and it was under this tenure, with that of Cornage, and sometimes with a combination of these forms, that most of the tenements of the manors of Cumberland and Westmorland were held. These holders came to be described as customary tenants. The customary tenant is distinguished from the freeholder, and the copyholder, in that he is not seised of his land in fee simple, as is the freeholder, and is not subject to the disabilities of the copyholder, nor are his customary dues considered derogatory to the nobility of his tenure. The customary tenant is therefore between the freeholder and the copyholder, with a number of well defined privileges. The two most important duties of the average tenant in Cumberland and Westmorland were those of warfare and the watching of the forests. The former depended entirely upon the attitude of the other kingdoms, especially Scotland; the latter was a long and laborious service laid upon the tenant until the middle of the XVIth century. The counties of Cumberland and Westmorland were dense forests until long after the Norman Conquest, and the timber for the royal ship-yards was grown in these highlands of England. The forests were full of game, and the regulations in connection with the preservation of game and the upkeep of the forests were most exacting upon the people.

From the middle of the XVIth century, however, these ancient laws and services began to lose their force, and a new set of regulations arose to meet the new environment. Slowly but surely the feudal system had passed away. Here and there a relic remained, but it was impossible to ignore the rights of men who could no longer be bought and sold with a tenement. From the first year of the reign of Elizabeth the border service is well defined and the claims of the tenants became fixed. Several years before, Lord Wharton, as Deputy-General of the West Marches, drew up a series of regulations for the protection of that part of the border. In an interesting article by Mr. Graham, we find how the men of Hayton, near Carlisle, turned out every night with their spears, and remained crouched on the river bank in the black darkness or the pouring rain. It is a typical example of borderers engaged upon their regular service. This system had superseded the feudal system. The feudal tenure survived in many instances where a power. Like one of their own tumultuous forces, when once directed into the right stream, they went to form that new product which we call an Englishman. The documents, which were discovered at Penruddock in the township of Hutton Soil—the "kist" is in the possession of Mr. Wm. Kitchen, Town Head, Penruddock—relate to a struggle between the lord and the tenants of Hutton John, Cumberland, on the subject of tenant right. So far as we are aware these documents are unique. The various authorities on Cumberland history give reference to a number of these disputes but no mention is made of the Hutton John case, so that we have here for the first time a full knowledge of what was probably the most important of all these trials. In addition, while there are no documents relating to the other cases, we have here every paper of the Hutton John case preserved. The story of the discovery is that the writer (the Rev. J. Hay Colligan) was searching for material for a history of the Penruddock Presbyterian Meeting House when he came across a kist, or chest, containing these documents. (A calendar of these documents may be found in the Cumberland and Westmorland Transactions for 1908.) The manor of Hutton John had long been in the possession of the Hutton family when it passed in 1564 to a son of Sir John Hudleston of Millum Castle by his marriage with Mary Hutton. Her brother Thomas had burdened the estate on account of his imprisonment lasting about fifty years. It was the son of this marriage, Joseph by name, who became the first lord of the manor, and most of the manorial rights still remain with the Hudleston family. After Joseph Hudleston came three Andrews—first, 1603–1672; second, 1637–1706; third, 1669–1724—and it was with these four lords that the tenants carried on their historical dispute. The death of Thomas Hutton took place some time after 1620 and was the occasion for raising a number of questions that agitated the manor for almost a century afterwards. It flung the combustible topic of tenure into an atmosphere that was already charged with religious animosity, and the fire in the manor soon was as fierce as the beacon-flare on their own Skiddaw.

The position of the parties in the manor may be summed up by saying that Joseph Hudleston insisted that the tenants were tenants-at-will, and the tenants on the other hand claimed tenant right. Whatever may have been the origin of cornage, it is clear that by the XVIIth century it was synonymous with tenant right. The details in the dispute cannot here be treated, but the central point was the subject of a general fine. This fine, frequently called gressome, was the entrance fine which the tenant paid to the lord upon admittance. In some manors it was a two years' rent, in others three. An unusual form in the manor of Hutton John was a seven years' gressome, called also a running fine or a town-term. This was the amount of two years' rent at the end of every seven years. The contention of the tenants was, that as this was a running fine, no general fine was due to the lord of the manor on the death of the previous lord. From this position the tenants never wavered, and for over seventy years they fought the claim of the lord. Upon the death of Thomas Hutton the tenants claiming tenant right refused to pay the general fine to Joseph Hudleston. After wrangling with the tenants for a few years, Joseph brought a Bill against them in 1632. He succeeded in obtaining a report from the law lord, Baron Trevor, which plays an important part in the case unto the end. He apparently disregarded the portion which applied to himself, and pressed the remainder upon the tenants. The tenants thereupon decided to send three of their number with a petition to Charles I. and it was delivered to the king at Newmarket. He ordered his judges to look into the matter. The civil war, however, had begun, and the whole country was about to be filled with smoke and flame. Needless to say the tenants took the side of Parliament, while the lord of the manor, the first Andrew, was described in the records as a Papist in arms. During the civil war the whole county of Cumberland was in action. The manor of Hutton John was mainly for the Parliament. Greystoke Castle, only two miles from the manor, surrendered to the Parliamentary troops. The termination of the civil war in 1651 was the date for the beginning of litigation between the Hudleston family and the Parliament on the subject of the manor. After this was over the struggle between the lord and the tenants began again. In their distress the tenants sent a letter to Lord Howard of Naworth Castle, whose Puritan sympathies were well known. This is a feature of the case that need not be dwelt upon, but without which there can be no complete explanation of the story. The struggle was in fact a religious one. The occasion of it was the entrance into a Cumberland manor of a Lancashire family, and the consequent resentment on the part of the adherents of the manor, who boasted that they had been there "afore the Hudlestons." The motives which prompted each party were those expressed in the words Puritan *v.* Papist. The year 1668 was a memorable one in the history of the dispute. In that year the tenants brought a Bill of complaint against the lord at Carlisle Assizes. The judge, at the opening of the court, declared that the differences could be compounded by some gentlemen of the county. All the parties agreed, and the court made an order whereby Sir Philip Musgrave, Kt. and Bart., and Sir John Lowther, Bart., were to settle the case before September 21st. If they could not determine within that time they were to select an umpire within one week, who must make his award before Lady-day. Sir Philip Musgrave and Sir John Lowther accepted the responsibility placed upon them by the court and took great pains to accommodate the differences, but finding themselves unable to furnish the award within the time specified they elected Sir George Fletcher, Bart., to be umpire. Sir George Fletcher made his award on March 3rd, 1668. The original document, written, signed and sealed with his own hand, is here before us. Its tattered edges prove that it has been frequently referred to. Sir George Fletcher's award was on the whole in favour of the tenants, and especially on the subject of the general fine, which he declared was not payable on the death of the lord. Other important matters were dealt with, including heriots, widows' estates, the use of quarries on the tenements, the use of timber, the mill rent, together with the subject of boons and services. All the tenants acquiesced in the award, and the lord paid the damages for false imprisonment to several of the tenants.

In the year 1672 Andrew Hudleston the first died, and Andrew the second, 1637–1706, succeeded to the lordship. He immediately began to encroach. He demanded the general fine in addition to rents and services, contrary to the award. The struggle therefore broke out afresh as fiercely as ever, and both parties returned to the old subject of tenure. The matter became a religious one owing to the Restoration and the rigid acts which followed between 1662–1689. An extraordinary incident occurred at this time in the conversion of the lord to the protestant cause, but this did not affect the dispute between him and the tenants. In 1699 the tenants moved again. They requested the court to put into operation the award of Sir George Fletcher. From that year until 1704 the strife was bitterer than ever, and the kist contains more documents relating to this period than to any other. In the year 1704, after several judgments had previously been made against the third Andrew Hudleston and his late father, the former appealed to the House of Lords, and the case was dismissed in favour of the tenants.

Although the struggle lasted until the year 1716, the climax was reached in 1704. The historical value of the case is the way in which it illustrates the conditions of tenure in the North-West of England, and at the same time pourtrays the pertinacity in spite of serious obstacles of the yeoman class in asserting its rights.

Tithe. The subject of Tithe is one that can only be dealt with in a restricted way and from one point of view. It is well known that, through the influence of George Fox in North Lancashire, Quakerism spread with frenzied force through Westmorland and Cumberland. Many of those who had been previously content with Puritan doctrines seceded to the Quakers. The practice of declining to pay the tithe, in the case which the documents before us illustrate, was of a different character. It occurs in the parish of Greystoke, in which the manor of Hutton John was situated. Five years after the award of Sir George Fletcher on the tenure case, the nonconforming section of the tenants of Hutton John raised another question of a tithe called "Bushel Corn."

This had been regularly paid to the Rector of Greystoke from time immemorial. Even the Puritan rectors had received this tithe down to that great Puritan, Richard Gilpin, who was ejected from the Rectory of Greystoke in 1661. The point in dispute was not a deliberate refusal of the tithe, it was a declaration of the parishioners that the *measure* was an unjust one. The contest was carried on by John Noble, of Penruddock, and Thos. Parsons, the steward of the Countess of Arundel and Surrey, Lady of the Barony of Greystoke. Associated with Parsons was John Robson, a servant and proctor of the rector. Parsons and Robson were farmers of the tithe, but the case had the full consent of the rector, the Rev. Allan Smallwood, D.D.

The immediate cause of the dispute was the question of the customary measure. It resulted in the settlement of a vexatious subject which was as to the size of a *bushel*. The matter was one of contention throughout the country until standard weights and measures were recognised and adopted. In Cumberland the most acute form was upon the subject of the corn bushel. The deviations in quantity were difficult to suppress, and several law cases upon this matter are on record. In the Parish of Greystoke the case was first begun in 1672. The bushel measure had been gradually increased from sixteen gallons, which amount the parishioners acknowledged and were prepared to pay, until it reached twenty-two gallons. The case passed through the assizes of three counties, being held at Carlisle, Lancaster and Appleby, and a verdict for the parishioners was eventually given.

The documents, apart from their intrinsic worth, have thus an inestimable value, in that they shed light upon and give information in regard to the doings in a

Cumberland manor where hitherto there has been but darkness and silence, as far as the records of the people were concerned. We are able now to follow with interest and satisfaction a story that is equal in courage and persistence with the best traditions of English love of justice and fair play.

The documents in this case were numerous but small, and were in many cases letters and scraps of paper. As a piece of local history it is not to be compared with the tenure case, but it contains valuable items of parish life in the XVIIth century. Perhaps the best of the letters are those from Sir John Otway, the well-known lawyer. John Noble the yeoman has several letters full of fine touches. The depositions of the witnesses at Cockermouth in 1672 are picturesque. The lawyers' bills, of which there are many, are not so illuminating. There are several letters of Henry Johnes of Lancaster, who was Mayor of that town on two occasions.

Public men regard it as a great honour to represent the northern districts of England in Parliament, merely from the intelligent political character of the voters; and it was certainly through the adherence of the love of freedom in the north that Cobden and Bright were able to struggle so successfully for the promotion of Free Trade and for financial reform. Sir E. Bulwer Lytton, the great English writer, says: "Those portions of the kingdom originally peopled by the Danes are noted for their intolerance of all oppression, and their resolute independence of character, to wit, Yorkshire, Lancashire, Norfolk, and Cumberland, and large districts in the Scottish lowlands."

Memorials of the Danes are mixed up with England's freest and most liberal institutions; and to the present day the place where the candidate for a seat in Parliament addressed the electors bears throughout England the pure Danish name of the "Husting." When William I. began to conquer England, and to parcel it out among his warriors, it was the old Danish inhabitants who opposed him; who would have joined him, their kinsman the Norman, especially as he gave it out that one of their objects in coming to England was to avenge the Danes and Norwegians who were massacred by Ethelred, but the Normans aimed at nothing less than the abolition of the free tenure of estates and the complete establishment of a feudal constitution. This mode of proceeding was resented, which would rob the previously independent man of his right to house and land, and by transferring it to the powerful nobles shook the foundation of freedom. The Danes turned from them in disgust, and no longer hesitated to join the equally oppressed Anglo-Saxons. The Normans were obliged to build strong fortifications, for fear of the people of Scandinavian descent, who abounded both in the towns and rural districts. What the Normans chiefly apprehended was attacks from the Danes who, there was good reason to suppose, might come over with their fleets, to the assistance of their countrymen in the North of England.

The Norman kings who succeeded William the Conqueror dwelt in perfect safety in the southern districts, but did not venture north without some fear, and a chronicler who lived at the close of the twelfth century assures us that they never visited this part of the kingdom without being accompanied by a strong army.

Abolition of Slavery.

In those districts where the Danes exercised complete dominion the custom of slavery was abolished. This fact is established by a comparison of the population of those districts colonised by the Danes with that of the older English districts. The population returns given in Domesday Book prove that no "servi" existed in the counties where Danish influence was greatest. Both in Yorkshire and Lincolnshire at this time there is no record of slavery. In the counties where this influence was less, such as Nottingham, the returns show that one serf existed to every 200 of the population. In Derbyshire 1 per cent., in Norfolk and Suffolk 4 per cent., in Leicestershire 6 per cent., in Northamptonshire 10 per cent., in Cambridge, Hertford and Essex 11 per cent. Outside the influence of the Danelagh the proportion is much greater. In Oxfordshire 14 per cent. were slaves, in Worcester, Bucks, Somerset and Wiltshire 15 per cent., in Dorset and Hampshire 16 per cent., in Shropshire 17 per cent., in Devonshire 18 per cent., in Cornwall 21 per cent., and in Gloucestershire 24 per cent., or almost one-fourth of the whole population. These records were not made by Danish surveyors, but Norman officials, and explode the theory of historians like Green who assert that the English settlers were Communities of free men. These conditions of tenure were introduced by the Danes, and became so firmly established that the names given to such freeholders as "statesmen" in Cumberland, "freemen" and "yeomen" in Yorkshire, Westmorland and North Lancashire still exist at the present day.

As we have seen, records of struggles for tenant rights have come to light in recent years which prove that feudal conditions were imposed by successive landlords, and were resisted both before and after the Commonwealth.

Invasion and Settlement.

The Norse settlement at the mouth of the Dee dated from the year 900 when Ingimund, who had been expelled from Dublin, was given certain waste lands near Chester, by Aethelflaed, Lady of the Mercians. This colony extended from the shore of Flint, over the Wirral peninsula to the Mersey, and it is recorded in Domesday by the name of their Thingwall or Tingvella. Along with the group of Norse names in the Wirral is Thurstaston, or Thors-Stone, or Thorstun-tun. This natural formation of red sandstone has been sometimes mistaken for a Tingmount or Norse monument. Several monuments of the tenth century Norse colony are to be found in the district, such as the Hogback Stone in West Kirby Museum, and the gravestone bearing the wheel-shaped head. A similar monument was found on Hilbre Island, and other remains of cross slabs occur at Neston and Bromborough.

The Norse place-names of Wirral prove that these lands were waste and unoccupied, when names of Danish origin were given, such as Helsby, Frankby, Whitby, Raby, Irby, Greasby and Pensby. Some Wirral names are composed of Celtic and Norse, as the settlers brought both Gælic and Norse names from Ireland. These are found in the Norse Runes in the Isle of Man and north of Lancaster.

Socmen were manorial tenants who were free in status, though their land was not held by charter, like that of a freeholder, but was secured to them by custom. They paid a fixed rent for the virgate, or part of a virgate, which they generally held; and, taking the Peterborough Socmen as examples, they were bound to render farm produce, such as fowls and eggs, at stated seasons; to lend their plough teams thrice in winter and spring; to mow and carry hay; to thresh and harrow, and do other farm work for one day . . . and to help at the harvest for one or two days. Their services contrasted with the *week-work* of a villein, were little more than nominal and are comparable to those of the Radmanni. The Peterborough socmen reappear under the "Descriptio Militum" of the abbey, where it is said they were served "cum militibus," but this appears to be exceptional. Socmen were like "liber tenentes" frequently liable to "merchet, heriot and tallage." Their tenure was the origin of free socage, common in the thirteenth century, and now the prevailing tenure of land in England. Socmen held land by a fixed money payment, and by a fixed though trivial amount of base service which would seem to ultimately disappear by commutation." All socmen as customary tenants required the intervention of the steward of the manor in the transfer or sale of their rights. ("Palgrave's Dictionary of Political Economy," p. 439.)

Merchet. Of all the manorial exactions the most odious was the "Merchetum," a fine paid by the villain on giving his daughter in marriage. It was considered as a mark of servile descent, and the man free by blood was supposed to be always exempted from it, however debased his position was in every other respect.

In the status of socmen, developed from the law of Saxon freemen there was usually nothing of the kind. "Heriot" was the fine or tax payable to the lord or abbot on the death of the socman. The true Heriot is akin in name and in character to the Saxon "here-great"—to the surrender of the military outfit supplied by the chief to his follower. In feudal time and among peasants it is not the war-horse and armour that is meant, but the ox and harness take their place. (Vinogradoff, "Mediæval Manors": Political Exactions, Chap. V., 153.)

Mol-men. Etymologically, there is reason to believe that this term is of Danish origin, and the meaning has been kept in practice by the Scotch dialect (*vide* "Ashley, Economic History," i, pp. 56—87.)

Tallage. The payment of arbitrary tallage is held during the thirteenth century to imply a servile status. Such tallage at will is not very often found in documents, although the lord sometimes retained his prerogative in this respect even when sanctioning the customary form of renders and services. Now and then it is mentioned that tallage is to be levied once a year although the amount remains uncertain. ("Villianage in England," Chap. v, 163, Vinogradoff.)

Husbandry

CHAPTER VII.

HUSBANDRY.

The influence of the Norse has been felt in terms connected with land. " God speed the plough " has been the toast of many a cup at many a merry meeting for many a century past in this realm. Yet we seem not generally to know by whom the name of the plough was introduced amongst us. The Anglo-Saxon knew nothing of such an implement and its uses ere they settled in the land. This is apparent from their not having a term for it in their own tongue. Even when they were accustomed to the use of the so-called plough of the Romans, which they found in the hands of the British at their settlement in the country, they so confounded the terms of husbandry that they gave the name of " syl " or " suhl " to the Roman-British implement, from the furrow " sulcus," which it drew, without attending in the least to the Roman-British name. The work of one such plough during a season they have called a " sulling " or furrowing.

This so-called plough, from the figures left of it in the Anglo-Saxon MSS., seems to have been but a sorry kind of an article, not fit to be brought into comparison with the worst form of our plough in the neglected districts of England. We owe both the framework and the origin of the modern plough to the Northerners. We meet with the word in the old Norse "plogr." In Swedish it is "plog"; while in Danish it occurs both as "plov" and "ploug," as in English, and it was in all probability introduced by that people during the eleventh century, at the latter part of their dynasty within the island. There is no root either in the Teutonic or Scandinavian tongues from which it is deducible. The British name for their plough was "aradr," their mode of pronouncing the Latin "aratum," the word for the Roman plough. The sort of agriculture which was known in the very early times must have been extremely simple, if we are to judge it by the terms which have reached our times.

Ulphilas, in his translation of the Greek Testament construes the word for plough with the Gothic word "hôha," the origin of our modern term "hoe." We may therefore surmise that in these primitive times natives hoed the ground for their crops for want of better implements to turn up the soil.

While we owe to the Norse the name for plough, we are also indebted to them for the term "husbandry." Among the Scandinavians, the common name for the peasantry was "bondi," the abstract form of "buondi," dwelling in, or inhabiting a country. As intercourse with more civilised nations began to civilise the inhabitants of these northern climes, certain favoured "bondi" had houses assigned to them, with plots of ground adjoining for the use of their families. As the culture of such private plots was distinct from the common culture of other land, the person so favoured, separated from the general herd, obtained the name of "husbondi," and the culture of their grounds "husbondri." When such families obtained settlements in England, they brought over with them the habits and names of the North; and from mingling with the Anglo-Saxon natives, with whom adjuncts to introduced terms and titles were common, the suffix of "man" was applied to the name of "husbondi," who thus became "husbandmen," a term still kept up in the northern counties for labourers on farms, who are styled husbandmen to this day.

Names from trades and handicrafts were given to persons employed therein both by Danes and Anglo-Saxons. Such names keep up their distinction to the present day. The general name of artizans of every kind was Smith. Simple "Smiths" are Anglo-Saxon, "Smithies" are Norse. "Millars," from the trade of millers, are Anglo-Saxon. "Milners" for the same reason are Norse. "Ulls," "Woolley" is Anglo-Saxon, "Woolner" is Norse; "Fullers" and "Towers" are Anglo-Saxon; "Kilners" and "Gardners," Norse. Some names derived from offices as "Gotts" from "Gopr," a priest, or one who had charge of a "hof," or heathen temple in the north. "Goods" comes from "Gopa," and "barge" from "bargr."

As further instances we may notice the names of buildings. "Bigging," applied to a building, shows it to be Norse, as in "Newbiggin" and "Dearsbiggin." Such buildings were built of timber, and had an opening for the door and an eyelet for a window. In the Norse this opening was called "vindanga," or windeye, which term we have adopted, and modernised it into our word "window." We have also chosen several Norse names for our domesticated animals. "Bull" we have formed from the Norse "bole." "Gommer," or "Gimmer" we retain in the northern dialect for ewe lamb, from the Norse "Gimber." "Stegg," the name for a gander, is in Norse "Stegger. In the north nicknames were general, and every man had his nickname, particularly if there was aught remarkable in his appearance or character. Some obtained such names from their complexions, as the "Greys," "Whites," "Blacks," "Browns," "Blakes." Short and dwarfish persons took the nicknames of "Stutts," nowadays called "Stotts." Before Christianity found its way among the natives, some bore fanciful names, as may be instanced in "Bjorn," a bear, now "Burns." Prefixes to such fanciful names were also common, as in "Ashbjorn," the bear of the Osir or gods, in modern times spelt "Ashburns"; and "Thorbjorn," the bear of Thor, whence came "Thornber" and "Thorburn." The name of "Mather" is Norse for Man, and as Norse names are general, we may produce the following: "Agur" from "Ager"; "Rigg" from "Rig"; "Grime" from "Grimr"; "Foster" from "Fostr"; "Harland" from "Arlant"; "Grundy" from "Grunrd"; "Hawkes" from "Hawkr"; and "Frost" from "Frosti," which are of frequent occurrence in the old Norse Sagas.

In the Vale of the Lune the Danes have left numerous traces. North of Lancaster is Halton, properly "Haughton," named from the tumulus or Danish "haugh," within the village. These are the names of the "bojais" or farms belonging to "byes," or residences of their greatmen. Near Hornby we find such places at "Whaitber," "Stainderber," "Threaber," "Scalaber." Within the manor of Hornby are "Santerfell," "Romsfell," "Litherell," or fell of the hillside. The name of fell for mountain bespeaks Norse or Danish influence.

The Raven was the national symbol of the Danes. We have Ravenstonedale and Ravenshore, and we also find the name in Rivington Pike, from Raven-dun-pike. Pike is a common name for a hill or spur standing away from the mountain range, and is derived from the Picts. The derivation of our common pronoun "same" is to be traced through the old Norse "samt," "sama," and "som," and has been selected into our tongue from the definite form "sama," the same. While we might expect to meet with this word, in the Lowland Scotch, where the Norse influence was greater, the people use the Anglo-Saxon "ilia" or "ylea," while in the general English, where the influence of the Northmen was less, we have adopted the Norse word "same," to the exclusion of the word we might expect to consider as our own. Many a good word do we owe to the Norsmen, whatever we may think about their deeds.

Stone Crosses

CHAPTER IX.

Stone Crosses.

The Parish Church of St. Peter, Bolton, was rebuilt entirely by Mr. Peter Ormrod, whose surname is Danish, and was consecrated on St. Peter's Day, 1871. Among the pre-Norman stones discovered during the re-building were the broken head of a supposed Irish cross, of circular type, probably of the tenth century; part of the shaft of a cross bearing a representation of Adam and Eve, with the apple between their lips, and an upturned hand; and a stone with carving of a nondescript monster. At this period the Danes were the rulers of Ireland and the Isle of Man, whose Bishops were men bearing Danish names, and therefore we may assume that this memorial was erected under their influence and direction.

Some crosses, says Fosbrooke, in his Dictionary of Antiquities, owe their origin to the early Christians marking the Druid stones with crosses, in order to change the worship without breaking the prejudice. Some of the crosses presumed to be Runic rather belong to the civilised Britons, were erected by many of the Christian kings before a battle or a great enterprise, with prayers and supplication for the assistance of Almighty God. At a later period, not probably earlier than the tenth century, a Scandinavian influence shows itself, and to a very appreciable extent modifies the ornamentation of these monuments. It went even further, and produced a representation of subjects, which, however strange it may appear, are only explained by a reference to the mythology of that part of Europe. The grave covers, to which, on account of their shape, the name of hog-backed stones has been applied, appear to have occurred very rarely beyond the counties of Cumberland, Durham, York, and Lancaster, though some not quite of the ordinary type have been found in Scotland, as, for instance, at Govan, on the Clyde, near Glasgow. They developed ultimately, through a transitional form, into the coped stone with a representation of a covering of tiles, the roof of man's last home, and were a common grave cover of the twelfth century.

Stone Crosses.

In pre-Reformation times there was scarcely a village or hamlet in England which had not its cross; many parishes, indeed, had more than one. We know that at Liverpool there were the High Cross, the White Cross, and St. Patrick's Cross. While many of these crosses are of undoubted Saxon origin, others bear distinct traces of Scandinavian mythology.

Heysham Hogback.

North Lancashire Relics.

In the churchyard of Halton, near Lancaster, is the shaft of an ancient cross. In 1635 the upper part was removed by the rector, in order that the portion remaining might be converted into a sundial. On the east side are two panels, one showing two human figures, in a sitting posture, engaged in washing the feet of a seated figure; the other showing two figures on either side of a tall cross. This is the Christian side of a cross erected at a time of transition. On the west side is a smith at work with a pair of bellows. He is forging a large pair of pincers, as he sits on a chair. Below the chair is the bust of a man, or a coat of mail. Above him is a sword of heavy type, also a second hammer, a second pair of pincers, and a human body, with a "figure of eight" knot, intertwined in a circle, in place of a head, and an object at his feet representing the head. The half-panel above has reference to some event in the Sagas.

At Heysham, near Lancaster, also in the churchyard, is an example of a hog-backed stone, a solid mass six feet long and two feet thick, laid over some ancient grave. On the stone is a stag, with broad horns, and as it is not a reindeer it is said to be a rude representation of an elk. The scene on this side of the stone depicts an animal hunt. The termination at each end is a rude quadruped on its hind quarters. A fragment of a beautifully-sculptured cross is still remaining, evidently part of a cross which fitted into the socket of the stone.

In the churchyard of St. Mary's, Lancaster, was a fine cross with a Runic inscription, meaning "Pray for Cynebald, son of Cuthbert." This cross has been removed to the British Museum.

Other Ancient Remains.

At Whalley are three fine specimens of reputed Saxon crosses. Tradition says they commemorate the preaching of Paulinus in 625. Although they have no remaining inscriptions, their obelisk form and ornaments of fretwork were used in common by the Norwegians, Saxons, and Danes.

In Winwick Churchyard is a great fragment of a crosshead, consisting of the boss and two arms. On the arms are a man with two buckets and a man being held head downwards by two ferocious-looking men, who have a saw beneath them, and are either sawing him asunder or are preparing to saw off his arms. This evidently relates to Oswald, for he was dismembered by order of Pemba, and the buckets might refer to the miracle-working well which sprang up where his body fell.

At Upton, Birkenhead, is a sculptured stone bearing a Runic inscription. Dr. Browne takes the inscription to mean: "The people raised a memorial: Pray for Aethelmund."

At West Kirby is a nearly complete example of a hog-backed stone. The lower part is covered on both sides by rough interlacing bands, and the middle and upper part with scales, the top being ornamented with a row of oblong rings on each side, with a band running through each row of rings. The work at the top, which looks like a row of buckles, is very unusual. The stone, which is of harder material than any stone in the neighbourhood, must have been brought from a distance, and in the memorial of some important person, probably Thurstan, as we find the name Thurstaston in the locality. There is also at West Kirby a flat slab on the face of which a cross is sculptured. This is very unusual in England, though not rare in Scotland and Ireland.

At Hilbree, the island off West Kirby, there is a cross of like character.

Principal Rhys says that in the eleventh and twelfth centuries the Norsemen were in the habit of largely recruiting their fleet in Shetland and the Orkneys, not merely with thrales, but with men of a higher position. They infused thus a certain amount of Pictish blood into the island. The "Shetland bind"—Oghams distributed over the island, in such places as Braddan, Turby, Michael, Onchan, and Bride. The Norwegian language, says Mr. C. Roeder, was spoken practically from 890—1270; it was introduced by the Shetland and Orkney men, and from Norway, with which connection was kept, as shown by the grammatical structure of the Runic stones in the island, which falls between 1170 and 1230. It was the only language of the rulers, and used at "Thing" and Hall, resembling in this old Norman barons and their counts in King William the Conqueror's time.

The spirit of the Norsemen lives in the legal constitution of the Government, an inheritance that produced a free Parliament, and particularly in its place-names. The sea fringe, with its hundreds of Norse rocks, creeks, and forelands, and caves, have left imperishable evidence of the mighty old seafarers, the track they took, and the commingling and fusion they underwent in blood and speech, and their voyages from the Shetlands and Western Isles.

Some Human Remains.

Claughton-on-Brock, near Preston, is named Clactune in Domesday Book. The Danes have also left relics of their presence and influence as they have done all over the Fylde district. The late Monsignor Gradwell, a great student of local nomenclature and a Lancashire historian of considerable repute, wrote: "In Claughton the Roman road crosses the Fleet, a small brook in the Sixacre. About seventy years ago a barrow was found on the west of the New Lane, about half a mile south of the street. In it were found an earthenware urn containing the burnt remains of a human body, with some delicately wrought silver brooches, some beads and arms, a dagger and a sword. The brooch of fretwork was precisely similar to many ancient

Hammer.

Brooch.

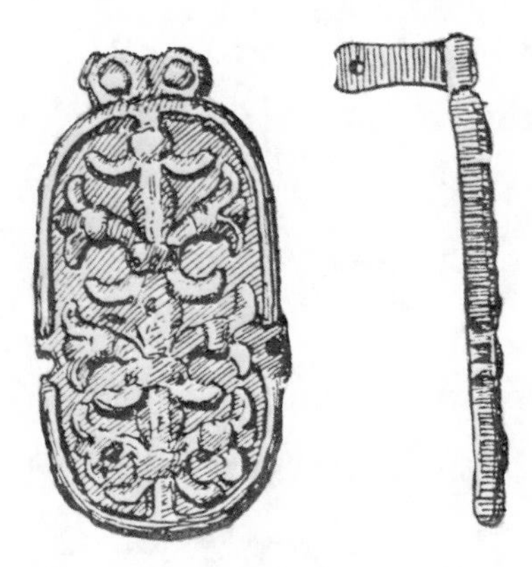

Fibula of White Metal from Claughton.

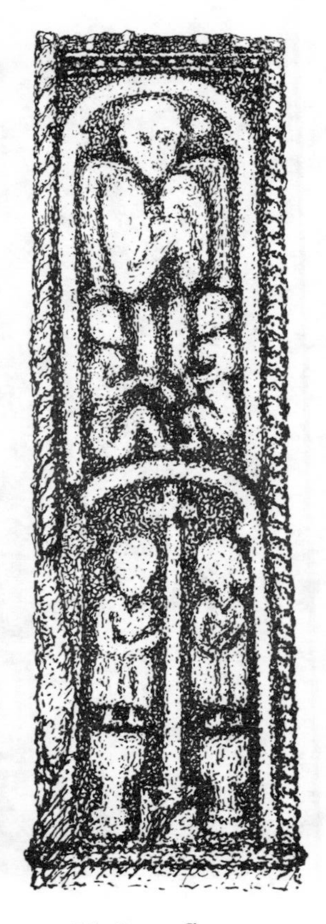

Halton Cross.

Danish brooches still preserved in the Copenhagen Museum, and this proves that the Claughton deposit was also Danish. That the Danes were strong in Claughton and in the neighbourhood is proved by the many Danish names. Thus, we have Dandy Birk, or Danes Hill; Stirzacre, and Barnacre, respectively Stirs land and Biorn's land. The Danish relics were carefully deposited at Claughton Hall by the finder, Mr. Thomas Fitzherbert Brockholes."

The Halton Cross.

Now what is to be said about the subjects carved on these crosses and about the date of the work? One of the subjects is most remarkable, and gives a special interest to this cross; for here on the west face and north we have the story of Sigurd Fafnir's bane; here is his sword and the forging of it, his horse Grani, which bore away the treasure; the roasting of the dragon's heart; the listening to the voice of the birds, and the killing of Regin the smith.

The story so far as it relates to our subject is this: We all know that the love of money is the root of all evil. Now there were two brothers, Fafnir and Regin. Fafnir held all the wealth, and became a huge monster dragon, keeping watch over his underground treasure-house. Regin, his brother, had all skill in smith's work, but no courage. He it was who forged the sword wherewith the hero Sigurd went forth to kill the dragon and take the treasure. This he did with the help of his wonderful horse Grani, who, when the heavy boxes of treasure were placed on his back, would not move until his master had mounted, but then went off merrily enough. This story, Anglicised and Christianised, is the story of our English patron saint St. George, the horse rider and the dragon slayer. Here is the story written in stone.

We know the ancient belief that the strength of every enemy slain passes into the body of the conqueror.

ILLUSTRATION OF HOG-BACK STONE.

The stone is perhaps more than a thousand years old, and has been a good deal knocked about. It was once the tomb of a great Christian Briton or Englishman, before the Norman Conquest; and you may still see four other "hog-backed Saxon" uncarved tombstones in Lowther Churchyard, marking the graves of the noble of that day. When a stone church was built, our sculptured shrine was built into the walls of the church, and some of the mortar still sticks to the red sandstone. When this old church was pulled down to give place to a new one this same stone, covered with lime and unsightly, was left lying about. You will see something twisted and coiled along the bottom of each drawing beneath the figures, and you will see some strange designs (they are sacred symbols used long ago) on either side of one of the heads in the lower picture; but what will strike you most will be the long curls of hair, and the hands pressed to the breast or folded and pressed together as if in prayer; and, above all, you will notice that all these people seem to be asleep; their eyes are closed and their hands folded or pressed to their breast, and they all look as if they were either asleep or praying, or very peaceful and at perfect rest. These people are not dead; look at their faces and mark generally the attitudes of repose.

Now let us find something worth remembering about all this.

The tombstone is made like a little house to represent the home of the dead. But at the time I am speaking of the people believed that only those who died bravely fighting would have a life of happiness afterwards; other people who were not wicked people at all—but all who died of sickness or old age—went to the cold, dark world ruled over by a goddess called "Hel," who was the daughter of the Evil one. "Such is the origin of our word Hell, the name of a goddess applied to a locality. Her domains were very great and her yard walls very high. Hunger is her dish, starvation her knife, care is her bed, a beetling cliff is the threshold of her hall, which is hung with grief." All, except the warriors who died fighting, however good, went to her domain. It might be thought that to be with such a goddess after death was bad enough, but there was a worse place. For the wicked another place was prepared, a great hall and a bad one; its doors looked northward. It was altogether wrought of adders' backs wattled together, and the heads of the adder all turned inwards, and spit venom, so that rivers of venom ran along the hall, and in those rivers the wicked people must wade for ever.

The Christian wished to show that this terrible idea of man's future state was to fire away to something better through the Lord of Life, our Lord Jesus Christ, and so they set up crosses and carried triquetra, the sign of the ever blessed Trinity, on their sculptured tombs to teach the people to believe no longer in gods and goddesses of darkness, but to look to one God, the Father, Son and Holy Spirit, to drive away all evil spirits from their hearts, and to give them a quiet time and a perfect end. Was there any wonder that years afterwards, when the bright light shone forth from the Cross to disperse the dark clouds of paganism, that men said that holy men, such as Patrick, Kentigern and Cuthbert had driven all poisonous snakes out of the land? The twisted and coiling thing beneath the figures is no doubt the old serpent. The Cross of Christ and the ash tree Yggdrasil of the northern tribes bore a like meaning at a certain time to the mixed peoples on this coast. (W. S. Collingwood.)

Anglo-Danish Monuments.

The great variety of ornament found in the North Riding Monuments shows that in four centuries many influences were brought to bear upon the sculptors' art, and much curious development went on, of which we may in the future understand the cause.

Our early sculptors, like the early painters, were men trying hard to express their ideals, which we have to understand before we can appreciate their work. The Anglian people included writers and thinkers like Bede and Alcuin, and that their two centuries of independence in the country of which the North Riding was the centre and heart, were two centuries of a civilization which ranked high in the world of that age. The Danish invasion, so lamentable in its earlier years, brought fresh blood and new energies in its train, and up to the Norman Conquest this part of England was rich and flourishing.

In writing the history of its art, part of the material will be found in these monuments.

The material of which these sculptures are made is usually of local stone. They were carved on the spot and not imported ready made.

In the progress of Anglian art we have the development which began with an impulse coming from the north, and ending with influence coming from the south.

The monuments were possibly executed by Anglian sculptors under the control of Danish Conquerors. Even under the early heathen rule of the Danes, Christians worked and lived, and as each succeeding colony of Danes became Christianised, they required gravestones, and Churches to be carved for them.

Following a generation of transition, at the end of the ninth century, monuments are found displaying Danish taste. The close connection of the York kingdom with Dublin, provides a reason for the Irish influence. Abundant evidence is found in the chain pattern, and ring patterns, the dragons, and wheelheads, which are hacked and not finished into a rounded surface by chiselling.

The Brompton hogbacks are among the finest works of this period.

The Stainton bear, and the Wycliffe bear, are also of this period.

The Pickhill hogback has an Irish-Scandavian dragon, and other dragons are to be seen at Gilling, Crathorne, Easington, Levisham, Sinnington, and Pickering.

New influences came from the Midlands into Yorkshire, after the fall of the Dublin-York kingdom, about the year 950. One instance of this advance in the sculptor's art is to be seen in the round shaft, trimmed square above, at Gilling, Stanwick, and Middleton, which came from Mercia, and passed on into Cumberland, where it is to be found at Penrith and Gosforth. These latter have Edda subjects and appear to be late tenth century.

Gilling has a curious device, which may possibly

Base and Side of the Ormside Cup.

be the völund wing wheel, and völund appears on the Leeds cross, and also at Neston in Cheshire.

The Scandinavian chain pattern, frequent on the *stones* of the North Riding, and in Cumberland, is entirely absent in manuscripts. There must have been books at Lastingham, Hackness, Gilling, and other great monasteries, but the stone-carvers did not copy them.

The Ormside cup, on the other hand, has close analogies with the two important monuments at Croft and Northallerton, which seem to be the leading examples of the finest style, from which al the rest evolve, not without influence from abroad at successive periods. It is to relief work rather than to manuscripts that we must look for the inspiration of the sculptors.

In these monuments linked together we can trace the continuation of the Viking age style during the later half of the tenth century and the early part of the eleventh centuries. The stone carver's art was reviving, stones were becoming more massive, which means that they were more skilfully quarried, the cutting is more close and varied, and on its terms the design is more decorative and artistic, though still preserving its northern character among impulses and influences from the south. But there is no room here for the Bewcastle cross or the Hovingham stone. We have an example of this period's attempt to imitate.

It is probable that the stone carving was a

traditional business, began by St. Wilfrid's, and Benedict Bishop's imported masons, and carried on in a more or less independent development as it is to-day.

With the Danish invasion began a period of new influences which were not shaken off until after the Norman Conquest.

The interlaced work was abandoned in the tenth century by southern sculptors, remained the national art of the north. The Manx, Irish, and Scotch kept it long after the eleventh century, and so did the Scandinavians.

The Bewcastle cross in the Gigurd shaft of the cross at Halton in Lancashire, and if this development has been rightly described the Halton shaft is easily understood.

In the period covered by the eleventh century dials inscribed with Anglo-Danish names date themselves. Interlacing undergoes new development, becoming more open and angular, until we get right lined plaits like Wensley, it is better cut, as the later part of the century introduces the masons who rebuilt the churches and began the abbeys. No longer was the work hacked but clean chiselled, and intermingled with new grotesques; we find it at Hackness, in the impost, and in the fonts at Alne and Bowes, where we are already past the era of the Norman Conquest.

Anglian work of the simpler forms and earlier types date 700 A.D.

Full development of Anglian art, middle of eighth century to its close.

Anglian work in decline, or in ruder hands, but not yet showing Danish influence, early ninth century.

Transitional, such as Anglian carvers might have made for Danish conquerors, late ninth century.

Anglo-Danish work showing Irish influence, early half of the tenth century.

Anglo-Danish work with Midland influence, later part of tenth and beginning of eleventh century.

Eleventh century, Pre-Norman.

Post-Conquest, developed out of pre Norman art.

Recumbent monuments were grave-slabs, which may have been coffin lids, such as must have fitted the Saxon rock graves at Heysham, Lancashire, while other forms may have simply marked the place under which a burial was made. They are found with Anglian lettering at Wensley, another has been removed from Yarm, and those of the Durham district are well known.

The two stones at Wensley may have been recumbent, like the Melsonby stones. The Spennithorne slab bears crosses of the earlier Northumbrian type, seen again in the West Wilton slab. At Crathorne are two slabs, with "Maltese" crosses apparently late, all the preceding being of the fine style.

Levisham slab has an Irish Scandinavian dragon.

Grave slabs are found of all periods and styles. Shrine-shaped tombs are known in various parts of England, with pre-Viking ornamant. (W. S. Collingwood).

Runes

CHAPTER X.

RUNES.

Before dealing with the Norse and Danish antiquities of Lancashire, of which we have some remains in the form of sculptured stones, and ancient crosses, it would be profitable to inquire into the origin and development of that mysterious form of letters known as Runes or Runic. How many of the thousands who annually visit the Isle of Man are aware that the island contains a veritable museum of Runic historical remains? A brief survey of these inscriptions, which have yielded definite results, having been deciphered for us by eminent scholars, will help us to understand the nature of those to be found in our own county.

We are told by Dr. Wägner that Runes were mysterious signs. The word Rune is derived from rûna, a secret. The form of the writing would appear to be copied from the alphabet of the Phoenicians. The Runes were looked upon, for many reasons, as full of mystery and supernatural power. In the fourth century Ulphilas made a new alphabet for the Goths by uniting the form of the Greek letters to the Runic alphabet, consisting of twenty-five letters, which was nearly related to that of the Anglo-Saxons. The Runes gradually died out as Christianity spread, and the Roman alphabet was introduced in the place of the old Germanic letters. The Runes appear to have served less as a mode of writing than as a help to memory, and were principally used to note down a train of thought, to preserve wise sayings and prophecies, and the remembrance of particular deeds and memorable occurrences.

Tacitus informs us that it was the custom to cut beech twigs into small pieces, and then throw them on a cloth, which had been previously spread out for the purpose, and afterwards to read future events by means of the signs accidentally formed by the bits of wood as they lay in the cloth.

In his catalogue of Runic inscriptions found on Manx crosses, Kermode says that "of the sculptors' names which appear all are Norse. Out of a total of forty-four names, to whom these crosses were erected, thirty-two are those of men, eight of women, and four are nicknames. Of men, nineteen names are Norse, nine Celtic, three doubtful, and one Pictish." This proves the predominance of Norse and Danish chiefs to whom these monuments were erected. Runes are simply the characters in which these inscriptions are carved, and have nothing to do with the language, which in the Manx inscriptions is Scandinavian of the 12th Century.

To speak of a stone which bears an inscription in Runes as a Runic stone is as though we should call a modern tombstone a Roman stone because the inscription is carved in Roman capitals. Canon Taylor traces the origin of Runes to a Greek source, namely, the Thracian or second Ionian alphabet, which, through the intercourse of the Greek colonists at the mouth of the Danube with the Goths south of the Baltic, was introduced in a modified form into Northern Europe, and had become established as a Runic "Futhork" as early as the Christian era. The main stages of development are classified by Canon Taylor as the Gothic, the Anglican, and the Scandinavian.

The Rune consists of a stem with the twigs or letters falling from left or right. This is the most common form to be found, allowing for difference of workmanship, of material, and space. The progress in the development of the Rune may be observed from the most simple plait or twist, to the most complex and beautiful geometric, and to the zoomorphic. The latter has the striking features of birds and beasts of the chase, and also of men, many being realistic; and except the latter are well drawn. The forms of the men are sometimes found with heads of birds or wings. In addition to decorative work we find on three of the cross slabs illustrations from the old Norse sagas. On a large cross at Braddan is a representation of Daniel in the lion's den; and at Bride, on a slab, is a mediæval carving of the fall of Adam, in which the serpent is absent. Both Pagan and Christian emblems derive their ornamentation from the same source, "basket work."

Long after the introduction of Christianity we find the Pagan symbols mixed up in strange devices on the same stones, which were erected as Christian monuments. In the "Lady of the Lake," Sir Walter Scott gives an account of the famous fiery cross formed of twigs.

> "The grisly priest, with murmuring prayer,
> A slender crosslet framed with care,
> A cubit's length in measure due;
> The shaft and limbs were rods of yew."

> "The cross, thus formed, he held on high,
> With wasted hand and haggard eye."

Basketmaking is the parent of all modern textile art, and no other industry is so independent of tools. It is the humble parent of the modern production of the loom, and the most elaborate cloth is but the development of the simple wattle work of rude savages. Plaiting rushes is still the earliest amusement of children, the patterns of which are sometimes identical with the designs engraved by our earliest ancestors on their sculptured stones. Interlaced ornament is to be met with on ancient stones and crosses all over our islands. Ancient pottery also shows that the earliest form of ornament was taken from basket designs.

The Lough Derg pilgrim sought a cross made of interwoven twigs, standing upon a heap of stones, at the east end of an old church. This was known as St. Patrick's Altar. This is recorded by a certain Lord Dillon in 1630, who visited the island known as St. Patrick's Purgatory on the Lough Derg, in Ireland. The wicker cross retained its grasp upon the superstitious feelings of the people after the suppression at the Reformation. He says of this miserable little islet that the tenant paid a yearly rent of £300, derived from a small toll of sixpence charged at the ferry. This was probably the last of the innumerable crosses of the same wicker and twigs. (Lieut.-Col. French, Bolton.)

Runic Almanacs.

When the northern nations were converted to Christianity the old Pagan Festivals were changed to Christian holidays, and the old Pagan divinities were replaced by Christian Saints. The faith placed in the early deities was transferred to the latter. As certain deities had formerly been supposed to exercise influence over the weather and the crops; so the days dedicated to them, were now dedicated to certain Saints.

The days thus dedicated were called Mark-days, and as it may be supposed it became the office of the Clergy to keep account of the time and to calculate when the various holidays would occur.

Owing to the fact that many Christian feasts are what are called movable, that is, are not fixed to a certain date but depend on Easter, the reckoning was more difficult for the laity than it had been in Pagan times.

In those days the fixed holidays could be easily remembered. An ordinary man without knowing how to read or write could keep a list of them by cutting marks or notches on strips of wood.

The successors of these are called Messe, and Prim Staves. The Messe staves are the more simple—*Messe-daeg* means Mass day, and the stave only denoted such days. The Prim stave contained besides the marks for Sundays and the moon's changes.. Hence their name from Prima-Luna, or first full moon after the equinox. The Messe-daeg staves are frequently met with. They consist generally of flat pieces of wood about a yard or an ell long, two inches wide, and half an inch thick, and have frequently a handle, giving them the appearance of a wooden sword. The flat side is divided into two unequal portions by a line running lengthways. In the narrow part, the days are notched at equal distances, half the year on each side, or 182 marks on one side and 183 on the other. In the wider space and connected with the days are the signs for those which are to be particularly observed: on the edges the weeks are indicated. The marks for the days do not run from January to July and from July to December, but on the winter side (Vetr-leid) from October 14 to April 13, and in the summer side (Somar-leid) from April 14 to October 13. The signs partly refer to the weather, partly to husbandry, and partly the legends of the Saints. Seldom are two staves formed exactly alike. Not only do the signs vary but the days themselves. Nor are they always flat, but sometimes square, *i.e.*, with four equal sides: when of the latter shape they are called clogs, or clog almanacs.

They are called Cloggs, *i.e.*, Logg, Almanacks=Al-mon-aght, viz., the regard or observation of all the Moons, because by means of these squared sticks, says Verstegan, they could certainly tell when the new Moons, full Moons, or other changes should happen, and consequently Easter and the other movable feasts. They are called by the Danes Rim-stocks, not only because the Dominical letters were anciently expressed on them in Runic characters, but also because the word Rimur anciently signified a Calendar. By the Norwegians with whom they are still in use, they are called Prim-staves, and for this reason, the principal and most useful thing inscribed on them being the prime or golden number, whence the changes of the moon are understood, and also as they were used as walking sticks, they were most properly called Prim-staves.

The origin of these Runic or Clog-calendars was Danish (vide Mr. J. W. Bradley, M.A., Salt Library, Stafford). They were unknown in the South, and only known by certain gentry in the North. They are quite unknown in Ireland and Scotland,

and are only known from the few examples preserved in the Museums.

Owing to the changes of custom in modern times these wooden perpetual almanacs have become quite superseded by the printed annuals.

The inscriptions read proceeding from the right hand side of the notches, are marks or symbols of the festivals expressed in a kind of hieroglyphic manner, pointing out the characteristics of the Saints, against whose festivals they are placed, others the manner of their Martyrdom; others some remarkable fact in their lives; or to the work or sport of the time when the feasts were kept.

Thus on January 13 the Feast of St. Hiliary is denoted by a Cross or Crozier, the badge of a Bishop.

Explanation of the Clog Almanac.

The edges of the staff are notched chiefly with simple angular indentations ΛΛ but occasionally with other marks to denote the date of certain special Festivals.

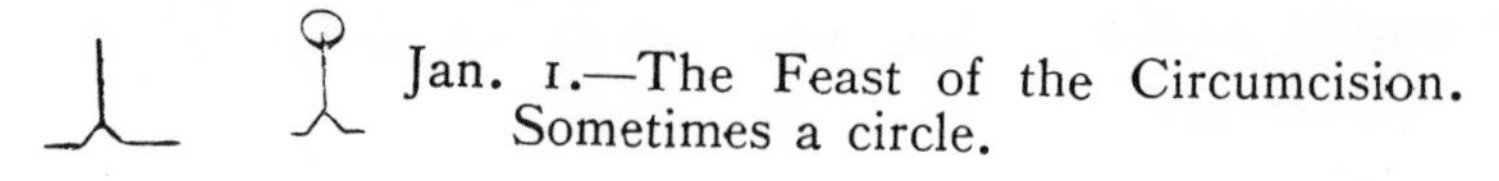

Jan. 1.—The Feast of the Circumcision. Sometimes a circle.

Jan. 2, 3, 4, 5.—Ordinary days.

Jan. 6.—The Feast of the Epiphany. Twelfth day. In some examples the symbol is a star ✱.

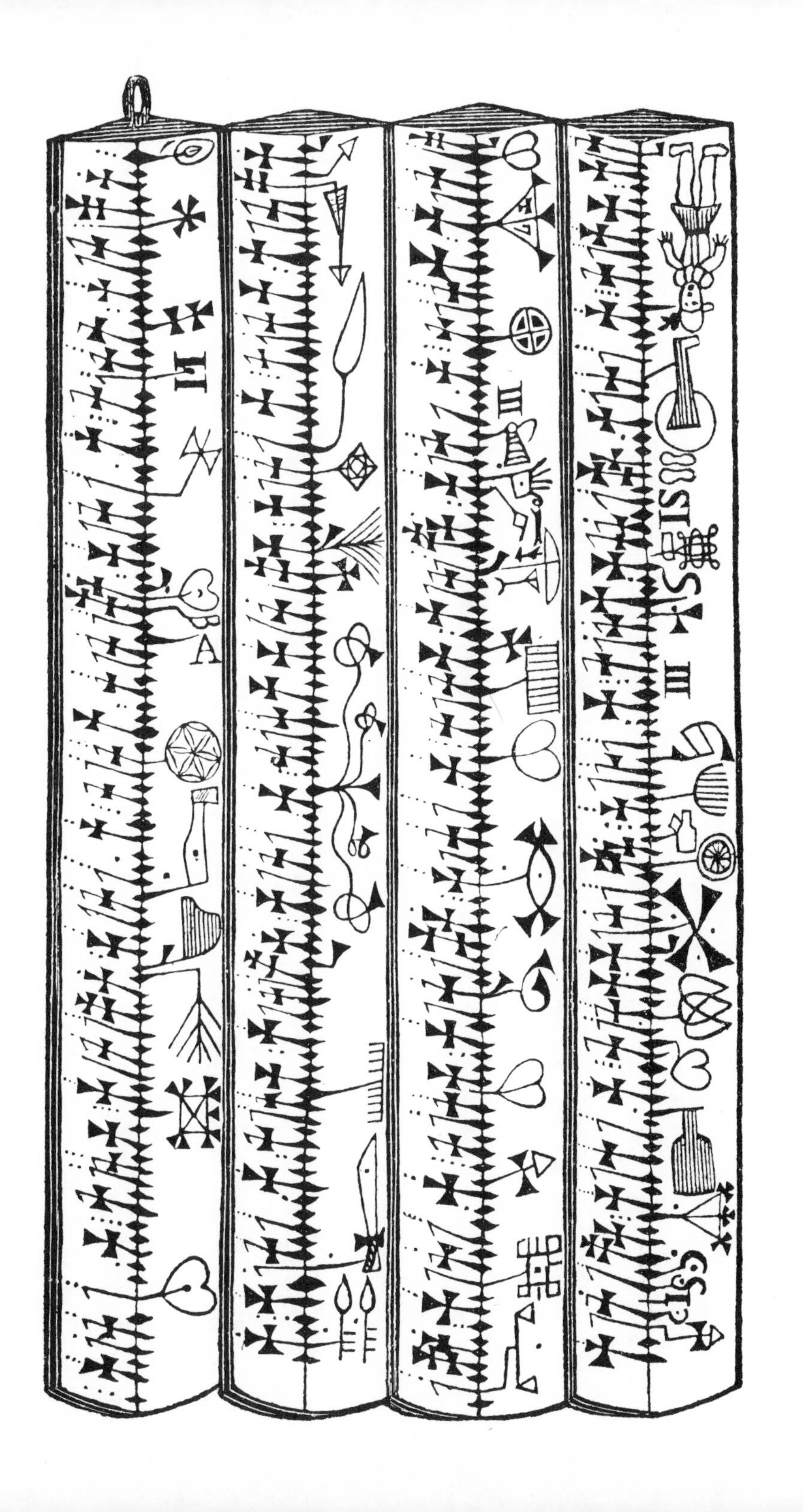

Jan. 7.—Ordinary day.

Jan. 8—12.—The first day of the second week is shown by a larger notch.

Jan. 13.—Feast of St. Hilary. Bishop of Poictiers, with double cross.

Jan. 14.—Ordinary day.

Jan. 15, 16.—First day of third week.

Jan. 17.—Feast of St. Anthony. Patron Saint of Feeders of Swine. This is the Rune for M.

Jan. 18.—F. of St. Prisca, A.D. 278. Not noticed.

Jan. 20.—F. of S. Fabian. Not noticed.
F. of S. Sebastian. Not noticed.

Jan. 21.—F. of S. Agnes.

Jan. 22.—F. of S. Vincent. Not noticed.

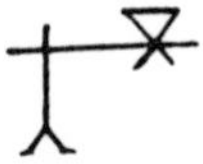

Jan. 25.—Conversion of St. Paul. Symbol of decapitation.

No other Saints days are noticed in Jan.

Feb. 2.—Candlemas. Purification of Virgin Mary.

Feb. 3.—St. Blaise, bishop and martyr. The Patron Saint of Woolcombers. Bp. Sebasti. Armenia. A.D. 316.

Feb. 4.—St. Gilbert. Not noticed.

Feb. 5.—St. Agatha. Palermo. Patroness of Chaste Virgins.
Feb. 6.—St. Dorothea. Not noticed.
Feb. 9.—St. Apolmia. A.D. 249. Alexandria.

Feb. 14.—St. Valentine (historian). M. A.D. 271. Plot gives

Feb. 16.—St. Gregory. Pope X. A.D. 1276.

Feb. 20, 22, 23.—St. Mildred, St. Millburgh, sisters.

Feb. 24.—St. Matthias, Apostle.

Mar. 1.—St. David, Bishop. Symbol a harp. Patron Saint of Wales. A.D. 544.

Mar. 2.—St. Chad. A.D. 672.

Mar. 12.—St. Gregory the Great. A.D. 604.

Mar. 17.—S. Patrick, Patron of Ireland.
Mar. 20.—S. Cuthbert. Not noticed.
Mar. 21.—S. Benedict. Not noticed. A.D. 543.

Mar. 25.—Feast of Annunciation. Blessed Virgin Mary. Usual symbol heart.

These complete one edge of the staff.

Thus each edge contains three months or one quarter of the year.

Turning the staff over towards the reader who holds the loop or ring in the right hand.

April 1.—All Fools Day. Custom. Not noticed. S. Hugh. A.D. 1132.

April 2, 3.—S. Francis of Paula. A.D. 1508. S. Richard, Bishop of Chichester, A.D. 1262.

April 4.—St. Isidore, Bishop of Seville

April 5.—St. Vincent. Terrer Valentia. 1419.

April 9.—S. Mary of Egypt. Not noticed.

April 11.—St. Gultitae, Abbot of Croyland.

April 19.—St. Ælphege, Archbishop of Canterbury. 1012.

April 23.—St. George, Patron Saint of England. Of Garter legend.

April 25.—St. Mark. Alexandria. Apostle and Evangelist.

April 30.—St. Catherine of Siena.

May 1.—May Day. St. Philip and St. James the Less.

May 3.—Invention or discovery of the Holy Cross.

May 5.—St. Hilary of Arles. A.D. 449.

May 7.—St. John Beverlev. A.D. 721.

May 8.—St. Michael Archangel.

May 19.—St. Dunstan, Archbishop of Canterbury. A.D. 988.

June 8.—St. William, Archbishop of York. 1144. Note the W. on the line.

June 11. St. Barnabas, Apostle. Commencement of the Hay harvest, hence the rake.

June 24.—Nativity of John Baptist.

Turnover staff for rest of June.

June 29.—St. Peter, symbol of key.

July 2.—Visitation of S. Elizabeth.

July 7.—S. Ethelburgh.

July 15.—S. Swithin, symbol as A.D. 862. Bishop of Winchester. Shower of rain.

July 20.—St. Margaret.

July 22.—St. Mary Magdalene.

July 25.—St. James, Apostle the Great.

July 26.—St. Anne.

August 1.—Lammas Day.

August 5.—St. Oswald.

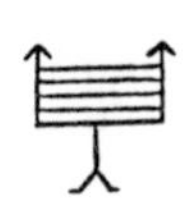

August 10.—St. Lawrence.

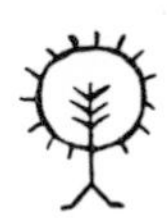

August 15.—Assumption of the Blessed Virgin Mary.
August 24.—St. Bartholomew.

August 29.—St. John Baptist.

Sept. 1.—St. Giles. Patron of Hospitals.

Sept. 6.—

Sept. 8.—Nativity of the Blessed Virgin Mary.
Sept. 14.—Exaltation of the Cross.

Sept. 21.—St. Matthew, Apostle.

Sept. 29.—Feast of S. Michael the Archangel.

Oct. 9.—St. Denis.

Oct. 13.—St. Edward the Confessor.

Oct. 18.—St. Luke the Evangelist.

Oct. 25.—St. Crispin, Patron of Shoemakers.

Oct. 28.—St. Simon and St. Jude.

Nov. 1.—All Saints.

Nov. 2.—All Souls.

Nov. 6.—St. Leonard.

Nov. 11.—St. Martin. Bishop of Tours, A.D. 397.

Nov. 17.—S. Hugh. Bishop of Lincoln, A.D. 1200.

Nov. 20.—St. Edmund, King of East Anglia.

Nov. 23.—St. Clement.

Nov. 25.—St. Catherine of Alexandria.

Nov. 30.—St. Andrew, Apostle.

Dec. 6.—St. Nicholas.

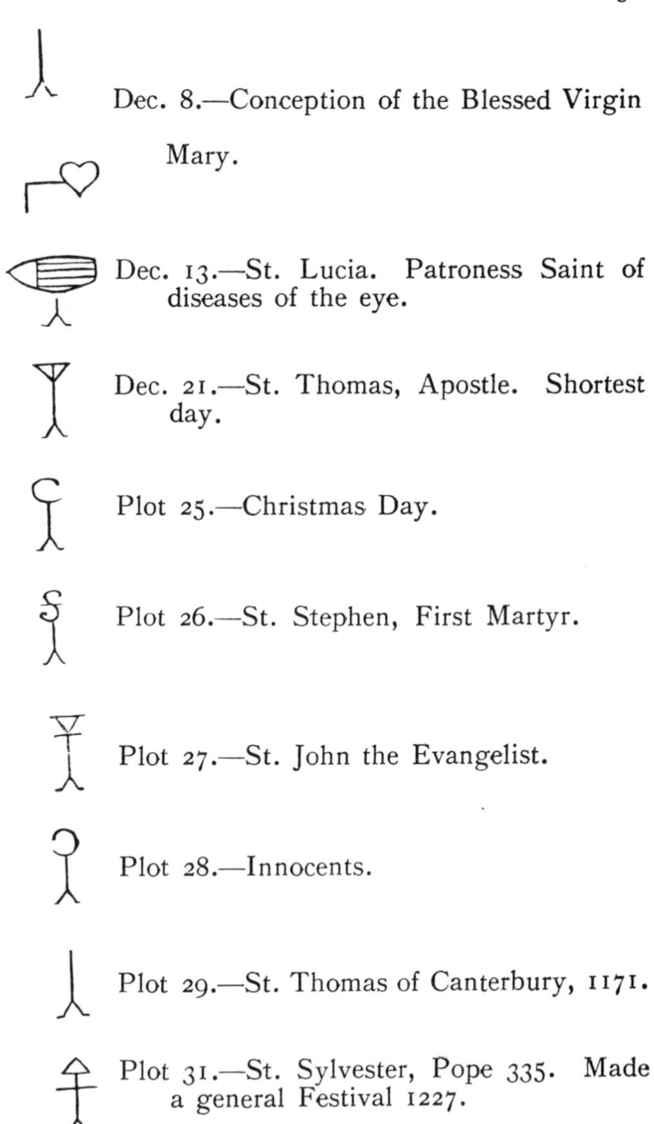

Dec. 8.—Conception of the Blessed Virgin Mary.

Dec. 13.—St. Lucia. Patroness Saint of diseases of the eye.

Dec. 21.—St. Thomas, Apostle. Shortest day.

Plot 25.—Christmas Day.

Plot 26.—St. Stephen, First Martyr.

Plot 27.—St. John the Evangelist.

Plot 28.—Innocents.

Plot 29.—St. Thomas of Canterbury, 1171.

Plot 31.—St. Sylvester, Pope 335. Made a general Festival 1227.

The more ancient almanac called Runic Primitare, so named from the Prima-luna or new moon which gave the appellation of Prime to the Lunar or Golden Number, so called because the Number was marked in gold on the stave. The Rim Stocks of Denmark so called from Rim, a calendar and stock a staff. The marks called Runic characters were supposed to have magical powers and so were regarded with dread by the Christians and were often destroyed by the priests and converts to Christianity.

They were derived from rude imitations of the Greek letters. Two of these staves now in the Museum at Copenhagen are 4 feet 8½ inches and 3 feet 8 inches long respectively. They are hand carved and not in any sense made by machinery. This accounts from them being rarely alike, and often very different from one another.

The Sun in his annual career returns to the same point in the Zodiac in 365 days, 6 hours, nearly. The Moon who is really the month maker, as the Sun is the year maker, does 12 of her monthly revolutions in 354 days. So that a lunar year is 11 days shorter than the solar, supposing both to start from the same date. The actual lunar month contains about 29½ days. Therefore in order to balance the two reckonings, it was agreed at a convention of Scientist Christians of Alexandria in the year A.D. 323, two years previous to the Council of Nice, to make the distances between the new moon alternately 29 and 30 days, and to place the golden number accordingly. Now these Egyptian scholars observed that the new moon nearest the vernal Equinox in 323 was on the 27th day of the Egyptian month Phauranoth, corresponding with our 23rd of March, so the cycle was commenced on this day. This is the reason why the golden number

1 is placed against it, 29 days from this brought them to the 21st April, and 30 days from this to the 21st May, and so on through the year.

Runic Calendar.

The explanatory engraving of the Calendar shows the year begins on the 23rd December. That this date is correctly given for the first day of the year is proved by the agreement between the Saints days and the days of the month on which they fall and the Christian Sunday Letters.

In thus beginning the year this Calendar exhibits a rare peculiarity. No other Runic Calendar begins the year in the same manner, while numbers could be shown which begin the year at Yuletide, commencing on the 25th December.

Of the two modes of beginning it there is no question that the one here exhibited is the genuine heathen while the other is genuine Christian. It is worth noticing that as Winter takes precedence of Summer in the sense of a year: so night takes precedence of day generally in the sense of a civil day of 24 hours in old Icelandic writers, a manner of speech which to this day is far from having gone out of use.

Considering the heathen tradition preserved in this Calendar in the number of days given to the year and in the date given to the commencement of the year, in which it stands unique, in the fact that the interval between 1230 and 1300, *i.e.*, out of 160 years rich in famous local and famous general Saints, not one should be recorded here: that Saints of universal adoration in the Catholic Church, such as St. Thomas of Canterbury, St. Benedict, and others, should not have a place here: we cannot escape referring it to an age when it may be fairly supposed that these heathen traditions were still believed in by at least a considerable number of the community.

Anterior to 1230 it cannot be, long posterior to that date it can scarcely be. That it must be a layman's Calendar, is shown because it exhibits no golden numbers, and gives consequently no clue to the Paschal cycle or movable feasts. It is a very valuable piece of antiquity and ought to be well taken care of.

On 2nd February were anciently observed all over the Pagan north certain rites connected with the worship of fire. In some places the toast or bumper of the fire was drunk by the whole family kneeling round the fire, who at the same time offered grain or beer to the flames on the hearth. This was the so-called Eldborgs-skäl, the toast of fire salvage, a toast which was meant to avert disaster by fire for the coming year.

Fire and Sun worship mingled together, no doubt in observance of this feast: for where it was most religiously observed amongst the Swedes it was called Freysblôt and was a great event. In early Christian times only wax candles which had received

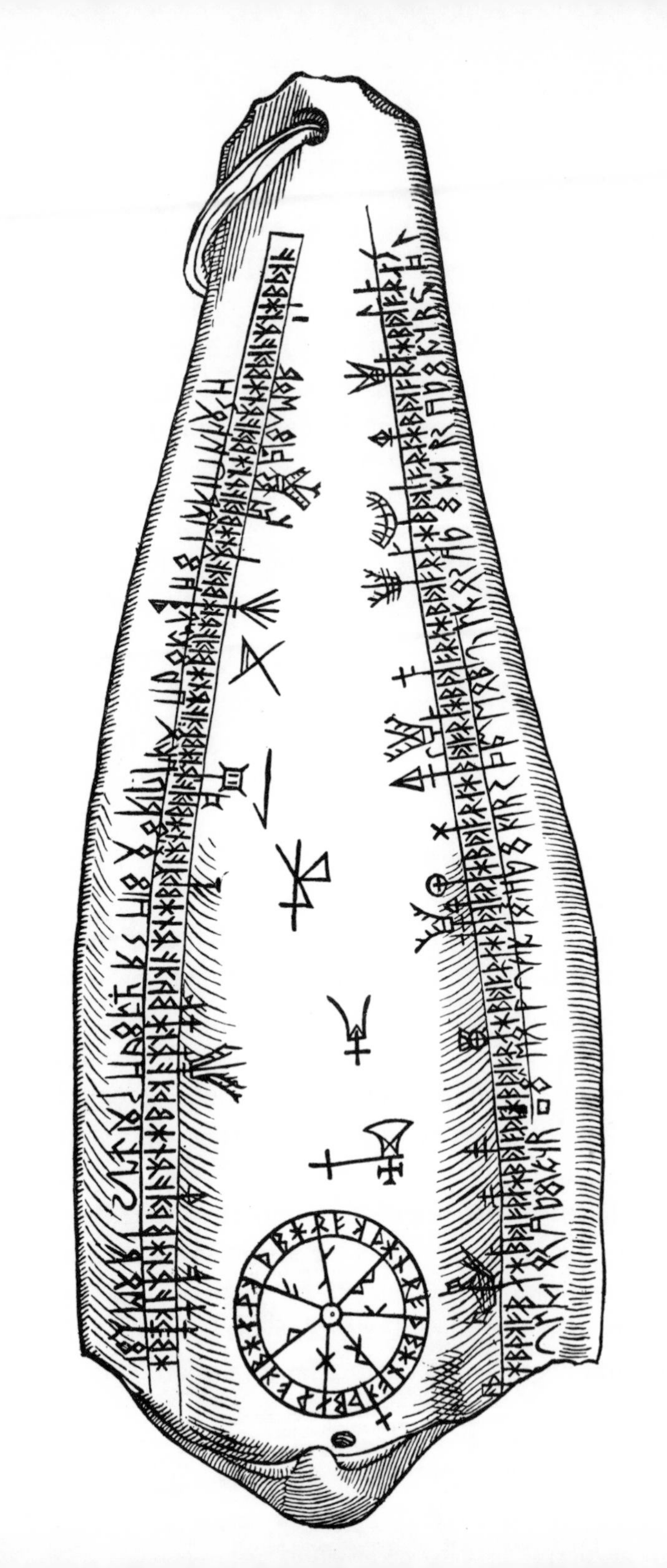

the blessing of the priest, were burnt in the houses of the people, in the evening. Hence Candlemas,—see illustration in Stephens' Scandinavian Monuments. From a remarkable treatise by Eirikr Magnusson, M.A., on a Runic Calendar found in Lapland in 1866, bearing English Runes. (Cambridge Antiq. Soc. Communications, Vol. X., No. 1, 1877.)

This English (?) or Norwegian Runic Calendar is dated about A.D. 1000—1100.

What distinguishes this piece is that seemingly from its great age and its having been *made in England*, it has preserved in the outer or lower lines several of *the olden Runes*. These are the "Notae Distortae" spoken of by Worm. Some of these as we can plainly see are provincial *English* varieties of the old northern Runes.

The Calendar before us is of bone, made from the jaw-bone of the porpoise. We know nothing of its history. Worm says, "Probably to this class must be assigned the peculiar Calendar carved on a concave bone, part of the jaw-bone of some large fish." Although it shows three rows of marks the signs of Festivals, the Solar Cycle and the Lunar Cycle, this last is here very imperfect and has even some distorted marks as we see in the engraving.

Each side, the concave as well as the convex, bears near the edge its girdling three rows of marks, so that every series comprehends a quarter of a year, beginning with the day of Saint Calixtus. As Worm has only given one side of this curious Rune-blade, we cannot know the peculiarities of the other half, which contained the Solar Cycle, and the three sign lines for two quarters.

On the side given, the Runes on the right hand are reversed and read from top to bottom; those on the left hand are not retrograde. It may often have been carried on the person, being only 18 inches long. The clog calendars range in length from 3 to 4 feet, to as many inches.

Whenever we light upon any kind of *Runic* pieces, we are at once confined *to the north*, Scandinavia and England. Though so numerous in the Northern lands, no Runic Calendar has ever yet been found in any Saxon or German province, except a couple bought or brought by modern travellers, as curiosities from Scandinavia.

Stephens says this whole class of Antiquities has never yet been properly treated. It offers work for one man's labours during a long time and many journeys. It would produce a rich harvest as to the signs and symbols, and Runes as modified by local use and clannish custom. All the symbol marks should be treated in parallel groups. The various and often peculiar Runes should be carefully collected and elucidated. All this is well worthy of a competent Rune-Smith, Computist, and Ecclesiologist. On many of the *old* Runic Calendars, especially in Sweden, we find a "*lake*" or game long famous all over Europe, but now mostly known to children, called "the Lake" or game of Saint Peter. This is an ingenious way of so placing 30 persons, that we may save one half from death or imprisonment, by taking out each ninth man as a victim, till only one half the original number is left. These 15 are thus all rescued. Of course the man thus taken must not be counted a second time.

Formerly the favoured 15 were called Christians and the other Jews. Carving this in one line, we get the marks so often found on Rune-clogs:

xxxx|||||xx|xxx|x||xx|||x||xx|

The story about it is this: Saint Peter is said to have been at sea in a ship in which were 30 persons, the one half Christians and the other half Jews. But a storm arose so furious that the vessel had to be lightened, and it was resolved to throw overboard half the crew. Saint Peter then ranged them in the order we see, every ninth man was taken out. The crosses betoken the Christians and the strokes the Jews. In this way all the Jews were cast into the deep while all the Christians remained. Herewith the old were wont to amuse themselves.

Folk-lore of children in rhyme and ritual. The child is surrounded by an ancient circle of ritualism and custom. Visitors to see the infant must take it a threefold gift. In some districts in Yorkshire the conditions are a little tea, sugar, and oven-cake.

Another Yorkshire practice is to take an egg, some salt, and a piece of silver. The child must not be brought downstairs to see the visitor, for to bring it downstairs would be to give it a start in life in the wrong direction. The form of this idea is to be found in certain (Japanese) customs. The child's finger-nails must not be cut with scissors, for iron had such close association with witchcraft. The nails must be bitten off with the teeth. This practice survives in some adults, much to the disgust of their friends.

Of children's games, that known as "Hop-scotch" was originally a religious rite practised at funerals. It was symbolical of the passage of the soul from the body to heaven or the other place to which the ancients gave various names. The pattern which is drawn for the purpose of this game has been found on the floor of the Roman Forum.

Another game called "Cat's Cradle" was played by the North American Indians, and has recently found on an island north of Australia. When children could not play on account of the rain they recited a little rhyme which is still known to-day by the people of Austria and in the wilds of Asia. The game of "Ring o' Roses" is the survival of an old incantation addressed to the Corn Spirit. When the wind rippled across the cornfield the ancient harvesters thought the corn god was passing by, and would recite the old rhyme, closing with the words, "Hark the cry! hark the cry! all fall down!"

Sometimes the corn spirit was supposed to become incarnated in the form of a cow, hence the line in the nursery jingle, "Boy Blue! the cow's in the corn." When the boy donned his first pair of breeches he must pass through a ritual. He must be nipped. The significance of the nip was a test to see whether the boy in the new breeches was the same boy, or whether he had been changed by the fairies or evil spirits. This idea of a change by evil spirits might seem far-fetched, but so recently as 1898, in the records of the Irish courts there was a case in which an Irishman was tried for accusing his wife of not being the same person as when he married her, and of the woman being branded in consequence. Superstitions as to the cure of certain childish complaints survive in the cure for whooping cough, to take the sufferer "over t' watter." That is the only medicinal use of the river Aire, near Leeds.

Memorials

L

CHAPTER XI.

MEMORIALS.

At the time of the Conquest the population in some of the largest and most important cities is said to have been almost exclusively of Scandinavian extraction.

In the north the Norwegian saint, "St. Olave," has been zealously commemorated in both towns and country. This proves that churches were built and Christian worship performed during the Danish dominion, and that these Northmen continued to reside here in great numbers after the Danish ascendancy ended.

In the city of Chester there is a church and parish which still bears the name of St. Olave, and by the church runs a street called St. Olave's Lane. This is opposite the old castle and close to the river Dee. In the north-west part of York there is a St. Olave's Church, said to be the remains of a monastery founded by the powerful Danish Earl Sieward, who was himself buried there in the year 1058. Long before the Norman Conquest, the Danes and Northmen preponderated in many of the towns of the North of England, which they fortified, and there erected churches dedicated to their own sainted kings and warriors. Olave is derived from "Olaf the White," who was a famous Norse Viking. He subdued Dublin about the middle of the ninth century, and made himself king of the city and district. From this time Ireland and the Isle of Man were ruled by Norwegian kings for over three centuries.

It may therefore be inferred, by a natural process of deductive reasoning, that during this period the Danes were founding their settlements in Lancashire. Although we have no distinct traces of buildings erected by them, the names given by them to many places still survive. In these compound names the word "kirk" is often met with. This must establish the fact that the Danes erected many other churches besides St. Olave's at Chester and York. From Chester and West Kirby, in the Wirral district, to Furness, in the North, we have abundant evidence in the name of Kirk, and its compound forms, that many Christian churches were erected. At Kirkdale, Ormskirk, Kirkham, Kirkby Lonsdale, Kirby Moorside, and Kirkby Stephen Norman churches have superseded Danish buildings. Kendal was known formerly as Kirkby-in-Kendal, or the "Church-town in the valley of Kent." And further memorials here survive in the names of streets, such as Stramongate, Gillingate, Highgate, and Strickland-gate.

The name Furness is distinctly Scandinavian, from "Fur" and "Ness," or Far promontory. The abbot of Furness was intimate with the Danish rulers of Manxland, for he got a portion of land there in 1134 to build himself a palace. He was followed by the Prior of Whithorn and St. Bede. In 1246 the monks of Furness obtained all kinds of mines in Man, and some land near St. Trinian's. By the industry and ability of these monks Furness became one of the wealthiest abbeys in England, and thus were laid the foundations of one of the greatest industries in Lancashire, viz., the smelting of iron ore.

Literature

CHAPTER XII.

LITERATURE.

During that period when the Danes were making their conquests and settlements in the North of England, art and literature did not hold any high position in Europe. The fall of the Roman Empire gave a shock to the pursuits of learning which had not recovered when Christian art was in its infancy. The Northmen early distinguished themselves in the art of shipbuilding, and also in the manufacture of ornaments, domestic utensils, and weapons. This taste had arisen from the imitation of the Roman and Arabesque articles of commerce which they brought up into the North. Some Scandinavian antiquities have been discovered belonging to the period called "the age of bronze," and also the later heathen times, known as "the iron age." The Sagas record that the carving of images was skilfully practised in the north, and the English Chronicles provide records of richly carved figures on the bows of Danish and Norse vessels. The Normans from Denmark who settled in Normandy were first converted to Christianity, and early displayed the desire to erect splendid buildings, especially churches and monasteries.

Long before the Norman Conquest, the Danes devoted themselves to peaceful occupations. Several of the many churches and convents were erected by Danish princes and chiefs, in the northern parts of England, which have now been re-built, or disappeared; but their names survive to distinguish their origin. It has been said that these early buildings were composed of wood. This is proved from the work recently issued by Mr. J. Francis Bumpus, in his "Cathedrals of Norway, Sweden, and Denmark." The touching life story of the martyred Saint Olaf is there told. A wooden chapel was built over his grave about the year 1047. This became the centre of the national religion, and the sanctuary of the national freedom and independence. Trondhjem, says Mr. Bumpus, is the eloquent expression in stone of Norway's devotion to the beloved St. Olaf. Despoiled of much of its ornamentation by Protestant zeal, it retains in the octagon of its noble choir a true architectural gem, equal in delicate beauty to the Angel Choir of Lincoln.

The phrase "skryke of day" is common to South Lancashire, and is the same as the old English "at day pype," or "peep of day." "There is a great intimacy," says Dr. Grimm, "between our ideas of light and sound, of colour and music, and hence we are able to comprehend that rustling, and that noise, which is ascribed to the rising and setting Sun." Thomas Kingo, a Danish poet of the seventeenth century, and probably others of his country-

Example of Danish Carved Wood-work, with Runes, from Thorpe Church, Hallingdal, Denmark.

men, make the rising of the Sun to pipe (pfeifen), that is to utter a piercing sound.

Tacitus had long before recorded the Swedish superstition, that the rising Sun made a noise. The form in which our skryke of day has come down to us is Scandinavian. Grimm says, "Still more express are the passages which connect the break of day, and blush of the morning, with ideas of commotion and rustling." Goethe has in "Faust" borrowed from the Pythagorean and Platonic doctrine of the harmony of the spheres, and illustrated Grimm's proposition of the union of our ideas of light and sound by describing the course of the Sun in its effulgence as a march of thunder. Jonson regarded noise as an essential quality of the heavenly bodies—

> "Come, with our voices let us war,
> And challenge all the spheres,
> Till each of us be made a star,
> And all the world turned ears."

The noise of daybreak may be gathered from the fracture of metal, and applied to the severance of darkness and light, may well have sound attributed to it. The old meaning of "peep (or pype) of day" was the joyful cry which accompanied the birth of light. "Peep," as sound is most ancient, and a "nest of peepers," that is, of young birds, is now almost obsolete English. Milton, in "Paradise Lost," shows the setting Sun to make a noise from its heated chariot axles being quenched in the Atlantic. Once, at Creation, the morning stars sang for joy; but afterwards moved in expressive silence.

Ballads and War Songs.

As a consequence of the Danish and Norman conquests, a peculiar composition arose called Anglo-Danish and Anglo-Norman. These legends and war songs were produced by the Danish wars, and were the expressions of an adventurous and knightly spirit, which became prevalent in England. The most celebrated of them were the romances of "Beowulf," "Havelock, the Dane," and "Guy, Earl of Warwick." In the older romances of Scandinavian songs and sages, combats against dragons, serpents, and plagues are celebrated; in later romances of the age of chivalry, warriors are sung who had fallen in love with beautiful damsels far above them in birth or rank, and whose hand they could only acquire by some brilliant adventure or exploit. The heathen poems of the Scandinavian North are all conceived in the same spirit, and it is not unreasonable to recognise traces of Scandinavian influence in English compositions. In later times, even to the middle ages, this influence is still more apparent in the ballads and popular songs, which are only to be found in the northern or old Danish parts of England.

Many parts of the Edda or Sagas have been

founded on songs in honour of the gods and heroes worshipped in Scandinavia.

In Shakespeare's " Hamlet " the young prince is sent to Britain with a letter carried by his two comrades. But he re-writes the letter and saves his life.

In the original Amleth legend of Saxo Grammaticus the two companions of Amleth, carry a wooden rune-carvel. But he cuts away some of the staves and adds others, so that the letter now tells the British king to slay the messengers, and to give his daughter in marriage to Amleth.

In the " Historie of Hamlet," London, 1608, we read, " Now to bear him company were assigned two of Fengons' ministers, bearing letters engraved on wood, that contained Hamlet's death, in such sort as he had advertised to the King of England. But the subtle Danish prince, being at sea, whilst his companions slept, raced out the letters that concerned his death, and instead thereof graved others."

LAY OF THE NORSE GODS AND HEROES.

Step out of the misty veil
  Which darkly winds round thee;
Step out of the olden days,
  Thou great Divinity!
Across thy mental vision
  Passes the godly host,
That Brugi's melodies
  Made Asgard's proudest boast.

There rise the sounds of music
  From harp strings sweet and clear,
Wonderfully enchanting
  To the receiving ear.
Thou wast it, thou hast carried
  Sagas of Northern fame,
Didst boldly strike the harp strings
  Of old Skalds; just the same
Thou span'st the bridge of Birfrost,
  The pathway of the Gods:
O name the mighty heroes,
  Draw pictures of the Gods!

These fairy tales of the giants, dwarfs, and heroes, are not senseless stories written for the amusement of the idle; but they contain the deep faith or religion of our forefathers, which roused them to brave actions, and inspired them with strength and courage. These Sagas existed for over four hundred years, until they exchanged their hero-god for St. Martin, and their Thumar, for St. Peter or St. Oswald, when their glory in Scandinavia fell before the preaching of the Cross.

ART.

Previous to their conquest of England, the Danes are said to have been unacquainted with the art of coining money. They are said to have imitated the Byzantine coins, by making the so-called "Bracteates," which were stamped only on the one side, and were mostly used as ornaments. The art of

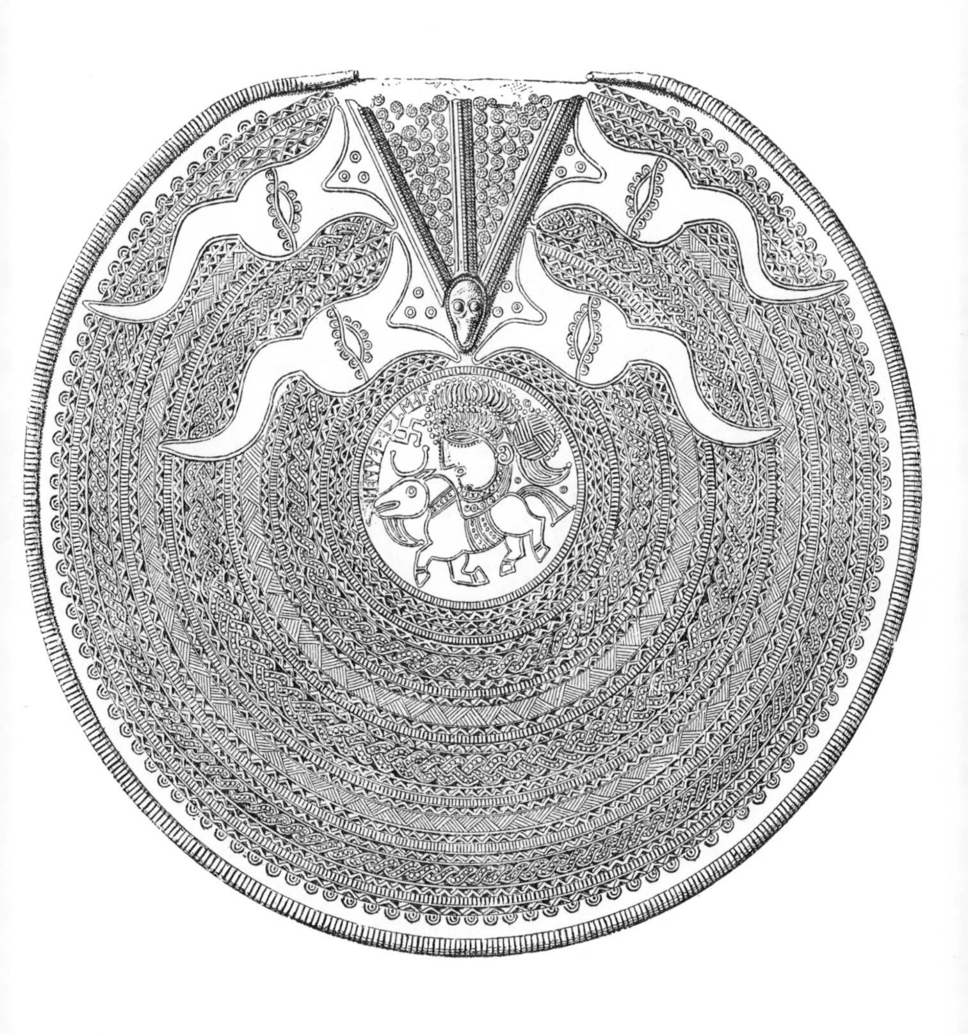

Bractaetes.

coinage was very ancient in England. It was the custom of the Anglo-Saxon coiners to put their names on the coins which they struck. In the eighth and ninth centuries the names of the coiners are purely Anglo-Saxon. But in the tenth century, and especially after the year 950, pure Danish or Scandinavian names begin to appear; for instance, Thurmo, Grim, under King Edgar (959—975), and Rafn, Thurstan, under King Edward (975—978); also Ingolf, Hargrim, and others.

These Scandinavian names are mostly found in the coins minted in the North of England, or in districts which were early occupied by the Danes. Under King Ethelred II., who contended so long with Canute the Great before the Danish conquest of England was completed, the number of Scandinavian coiners arose rapidly, with the Danish power, and the names of forty or fifty may be found on the coins of Ethelred alone. Even after the fall of the Danish power, they are to be met with in almost the same number as before on the coins of the Anglo-Saxon King, Edward the Confessor. These coins prove much and justify us in inferring a long continued coinage.

The great hoard of silver coins found at Cuerdale in 1840, some two miles above Preston, were buried in a leaden chest, near an ancient ford of the river Ribble. This treasure composed the war chest of the Danish army, which was defeated at this ford early in the tenth century, on its retreat into Northumbria. It contained nearly one thousand English coins of Alfred the Great, and some forty-five of Edward the Elder. The latest date of any of these coins being of the latter reign, the date of the hoard being buried may be fixed between the years 900 and 925. Many of the coins were continental, belonging to the coast of Western France, and from the district round the mouth of the river Seine. The appearance of this money agrees with the early records of the Saxon Chronicle, that of the year 897, which tells us that "the Danish army divided, one part went into the Eastern Counties, and the other into Northumbria, and those who were without money, procured ships and went southwards over the sea to the Seine."

The other Chronicle of 910 states that, "a great fleet came hither from the south, from Brittany, and greatly ravaged the Severn, but there they afterwards nearly all perished." It may be supposed that the remnant of this band became united with the main Danish army, and would account for the large proportion of foreign money. The bulk of the coins were Danish, minted by Danish kings of Northumbria.

From these circumstances, we may believe, this hoard to have been the treasure or war chest of this retreating army. This Cuerdale hoard is by far the largest found in Lancashire; it contained 10,000 silver coins, and nearly 1,000 ounces of silver

Halton Cup.

ingots. A smaller find, made at an early date, was the hoard of 300 silver pennies, discovered in 1611 at Harkirke, which lies on the sea coast between Crosby and Formby. Of this collection, some 35 coins were engraved at the latter part of the tenth century.

This engraving shows that these coins were minted by Alfred, Edward the Elder, and the Danish king Canute, and the ecclesiastical coinages of York and East Anglia. These coins were buried within a few years of the deposit at Cuerdale. We have numerous records of other Danish finds.

At Halton Moor, five miles above Lancaster, the discovery was made in 1815 of a silver cup of graceful design, containing 860 silver coins of Canute, with ornaments, which included a torque of silver wire. Mr. J. Coombe, of the British Museum, describes the coins as 21 Danish, and 379 of Canute. The latter being nearly all of one type, having on the obverse side the Head of the King with Helmet and Sceptre, and on the reverse a cross, within the inner circle, with amulets in the four angles.

The silver cup found on Halton Moor contained, in addition to the coins of Canute, a silver torque, which had been squeezed into the vessel. Both these silver articles are highly decorated and of great interest. The cup weighed over ten ounces, and was composed of metal containing three parts silver with one part copper. It appeared to have been gilt originally, some of the gold still remaining, which was of very pale colour. The ornamentation consisted of four circular compartments, divided by branches which terminated in the heads of animals, in Arabesque style. In these compartments are a panther and a butting bull alternately. This ornament is included inside two beautiful borders, which encircle the cup in parallel lines. The torque is of equal interest, and is a peculiar example of Danish wire-work metal rings, twisted and plated, with the ends beaten together for a double fastening. The face of this portion of the necklace, which is flattened, was decorated with small triangular pieces fixed by curious rivets. It was of pure silver and weighed six ounces six pennyweights.

Along with these deposits were some gold pieces, struck on one side only, with a rough outline of a human head. Similar pieces have been found in Denmark, and the Danish element is predominant in the whole decoration.

The Viking Age.

Before the Normans came our district was Scandinavian. From the year 876 they began to settle and behaved not as raiders but as colonists. They wanted homes and settled quietly down.

In the course of 200 years their descendants became leading landowners, as we see from the Norse names of the 12th century records.

Naturally the art of the district must have been influenced by such people: especially by the Scandinavians who had lived in Ireland, till then a very artistic country. Whether Irish taught Norse or *vice versa*, we see that there was a quantity of artistic work produced especially along the seaboard, and we are lucky in having analogies not far to seek.

In the Isle of Man the earliest series of Crosses have 11th century runes and figure subjects from the Edda and the Sigurd story which were late 11th century. Mr. Kermode, F.S.A., Scot., dates them 1050—1150 (Saga book of Viking Club, Vol. I., p. 369). We have them in the remains in Man a kindred race to ours in the age before the Normans came: and we find resemblances between these Manx Crosses and some of ours both in subject and in style. In subjects the 11th century Crosses of Kirk Andreas, Jurby, and Malew find a parellel at Halton, which Mr. Calverley places late in 11th century and attributes to people under strong Scandinavian influence: but Danish as it happens rather than Norse.

The Halton Crosses are not Norse in style. They are like the late pre-Norman work in Yorkshire where the Danes lived.

Then the Hogback stones have to be placed. We have fixed the Gosforth and Plumland examples by their dragonesque work as of the Viking settlement.

All these have the chain pattern, which Mr. Calverley called the Tree Yggdrasil or Tree of Existence, which shows that these monuments are of Viking origin.

From what models or pattern did these early sculptors copy their designs? It is sometimes said that they imitated MSS.: assuming that MSS. were fairly common and placed in the stone carver's hands. This is far less likely than that sculptors, at a distance from good models in stone, copied patterns from metal work which were the most portable, and most accessible of all forms of art, in the days before printing was invented.

Suppose, to make it plainer, the sorrowing survivor bids the British workman carve a Cross for the dead. "What like shall I work it?" says the mason. "Like the fair Crosses of England or Ireland, a knot above, and a knot below, and so forth." "But," says the mason, and he might say it in the 10th century, "I have never been in England or Ireland or seen your Crosses." Then answers the patron, "Make it like this swordhilt." (Calverley.)

The earlier Irish Christians were highly intellectual and literary, but not at first artistic. Literature in all races precedes art; it would be contrary to all historical analogy if Patrick and Columba had lived in the artistic atmosphere of the eighth and ninth century in Ireland. Patrick's bell is no great credit to Assicus his coppersmith: his crosier was a plain stick. There is no indication in our remains that Irish missionaries of the seventh century brought a single art idea into the country. It was the Irish Viking Christians of the twelfth century who did.

Mr. George Stephens, in his "Old Northern Runic Monuments of Scandinavia and England," vol. iii., under the heading "Runic Remains and Runic Writings," says:—

"I believe these stones, however altered and conventionalised, were all originally made for worship as gods or fetishes, elfstones, or what not, but in fact, at first as phallic sybols, the Zinga and the Zoni, creation and preservation, placed on the tumulus as triumphant emblems of Light out of Darkness, Life after Death. And the *priapus* and *cups* sometimes seen on burial-urns, must have the same meaning. Several of the grave minnes bearing old Norse runes were worship stones, carved with regular cups, etc., *ages before* they were used a second time for funereal purposes."

Prof. J. F, Simpson, M.D., Edinburgh, has a paper "On the Cup Cuttings and Ring Cuttings on the Calder Stones near Liverpool," in the Transactions of the Historic Society of Lancashire and Cheshire, vol. xvii., 1865, in which he states that—

"The Calder Stones near Liverpool afford an interesting and remarkable example of these cup and ring carvings upon this variety of stones—or, in words, upon the stones of a small megalithic circle. Some of the Calder Stones afford ample evidence of modern chiselling as marked by the sharpness and outray figurings. But in addition to these there are cut upon them, though in some parts greatly faded away, sculpturings of cups and concentric rings similar to those found in various parts of England and Scotland, remarkable for not only their archaic carvings, perfect and entire similarity to those found elsewhere, but still more from the fact that we have here presented upon a single circle almost every known and recognised type of these cuttings.

The Calder circle is about six yards in diameter, consists of five stones which are still upright and one that is fallen. The stones consists of slabs and blocks of red sandstone, all different in size and shape. The fallen stone is small, and shows nothing on its exposed side, but possibly if turned over some markings might be discovered on its other surface. Of the five standing stones the largest of the set, No. 1, is a sandstone slab between 576 feet in height and in breadth. On its outer surface, or the surface turned to the exterior of the circle, there is a flaw above from disintegration and splintering of the stone: but the remaining portion of the surface presents between 30 and 40 cup depressions varying from 2 to 3 and a half inches in diameter, and at its lowest and left-hand corner is a concentric circle about a foot in diameter, consisting of four enlarging rings, but apparently without any central depression. The opposite surface of this stone (No. 1) is that directed to the interior of the circle, has near its centre a cup cut upon it, with the remains of one surrounding ring. On the right side of this single-ringed cup are the faded remains of a concentric circle of three rings. To the left of it there is another three-ringed circle with a central depression, but the upper portions of the ring are broken off. Above it is a double-ringed cup, with this peculiarity, that the external ring is a volute leading from the central cup, and between the outer and inner ring is a fragmentary line of apparently another volute making a double-ringed spiral which is common on some Irish stones, as on those of the great archaic mausoleum at New Grange, but extremely rare in Great Britain. At the very base of this stone towards the left are two small volutes, one with a central depression or cup, and the other seemingly without it. One of these small volutes consists of three turns, the other of two.

The cup and ring cuttings have been discovered in a variety of relations and positions. Some are sculptured on the surface of rocks *in situ*—on large stones placed inside and outside the walls of old British cities and camps, on blocks used in the construction of the olden dwellings and strongholds of archaic living man, in the interior of the chambered sepulchres and kistvaens of the archaic dead, on monoliths and on cromlechs, and repeatedly in Scotland on megalithic or so-called "Druidical" circles.

The name Calder Stones is derived from Norse Calder or Caldag, the calf-garth or yard enclosed to protect young cattle from straying.

Norse and Danish Grave Mounds.

Amongst the ancient monuments of Britain the well-known remains called Druidical Circles hold a foremost place, though their use, and the people by whom they were erected, are questions which still remain matters of dispute. The Stone enclosures of Denmark, which resemble the Circles of Cumbria in many respects, mainly differ from them, in that they are found in connection with burial chambers, whilst the latter are generally situated on the flat surface of moors, with nothing to indicate that they have ever been used for sepulchural purposes. Therefore wherever no urns or other remains have been found, we have negative evidence that the place was not intended for a place of sepulture.

Cairns which are the most undisputed form of a Celtic burial place were once very numerous in the northern districts: but a great many have long since been removed. The graves of Norway bear an outward resemblance to the Celtic Cairn, but the

CALDER STONE No. I

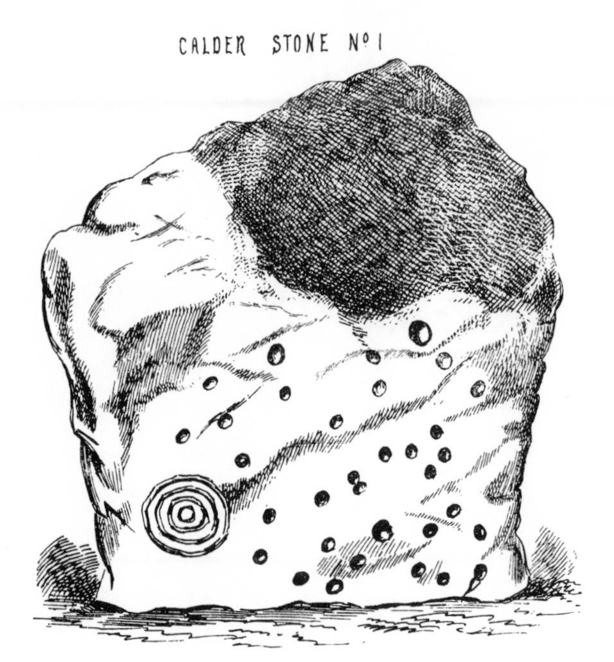

OUTER SURFACE.

INNER SURFACE.

CALDER STONE No 2.

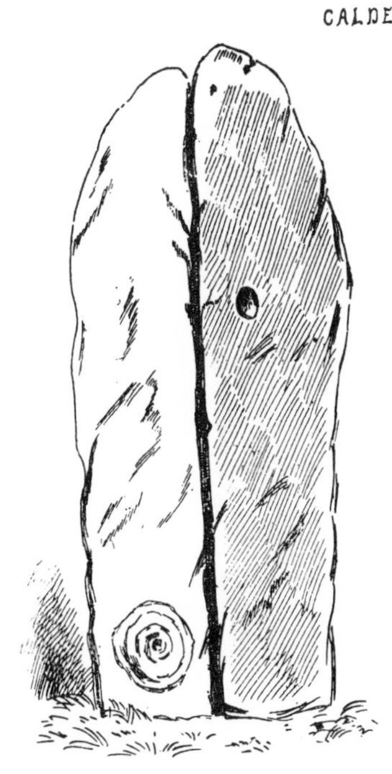

OUTER ASPECT, TWO SIDES.

INNER SIDE.

CALDER STONE No 3.

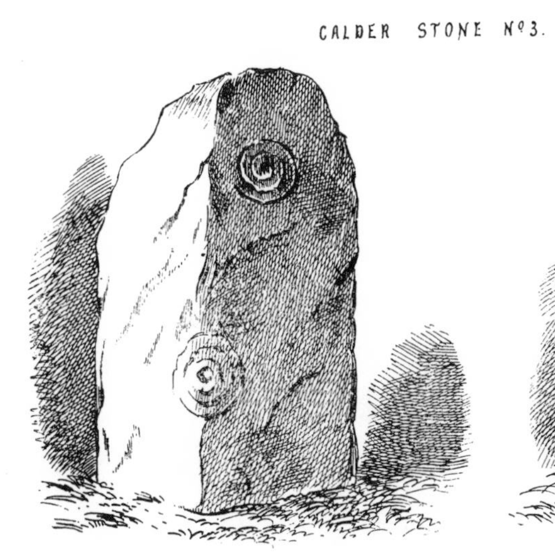

OUTER ASPECT TWO SIDES.

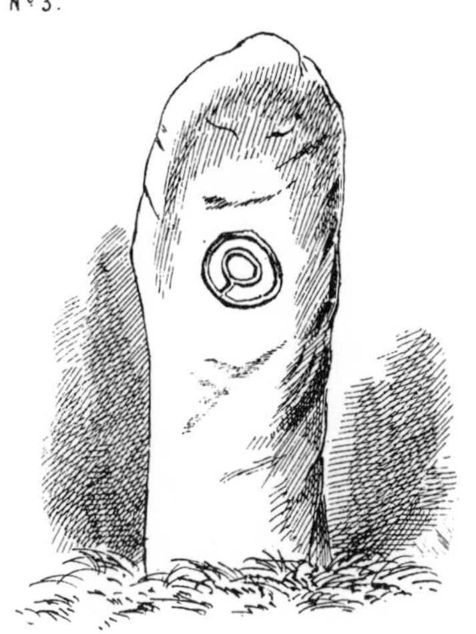

INNER SIDE

main cause appears to be that in mountainous countries stones are more easily procurable than earth. Where a doubt exists as to the proprietorship of these mounds, the only means of deciding is by an examination of the interior. The Norse Cairn should enclose a stone chest or wooden chamber and iron weapons. The Norwegians burned the body until about their conversion to Christianity.

Tumuli or barrows still remain in great numbers. As far as records have been kept of those removed, nearly all must be claimed for the Bronze age, and the main part of those yet standing are essentially of a Danish character. In the description of this class of graves, we have no actual mention of iron antiquities.

The Cairn called Mill Hill, Westmoreland, appears to have been a Celtic burial place, whilst Loden How was more probably Danish than Norse. Four different names are found in connection with sepulchres of this kind, viz., "how, raise, barrow, and hill," but the distinction is principally that of age, and the order of the words as here placed indicates the period to which each belongs.

Few traces of the Iron age can be regared as exclusively Norwegian wherever the body has been burned. Ormstead, near Penrith, was possibly a Norse burial place; while Thulbarrow, in the same neighbourhood, was in all probability Danish.

Memorial stones still remain in considerable numbers, the most remarkable of which is the Nine Standards in Westmoreland. Several villages called Unthank take their names from Monuments no longer in existence, the word being in English "onthink," and the phrase "to think on" is still current in the dialect.

Mythology

CHAPTER XIII.

Mythology.

The religious conceptions of the most famous nations of antiquity are connected with the beginnings of civilisation. We are told by Dr. Wägner, in his work "Asgard and the Gods," of the traditions of our northern ancestors, the story of the myths and legends of Norse antiquity. The first of their heroes was Odin, the god of battles, armed with his war spear, followed by the Walkyries, who consecrate the fallen heroes with a kiss, and bear them away to the halls of the gods, where they enjoy the feasts of the blessed. Later, Odin invents the Runes, through which he gains the power of understanding and ruling all things. He thus becomes the spirit of nature, the all-father. Then the ash tree, "Yggdrasil," grew up; the tree of the universe, of time, and life. The boughs stretched out to heaven, and over-shadowed Walhalla, the hall of the heroes. This world-tree was evergreen, watered daily by the fateful Norns, and could not wither until the last battle should be fought, where life, time, and the world were all to pass away. This was related by a skald, the northern bard, to the warriors while resting from the fatigue of fighting, by tables of mead.

The myths were founded on the belief of the Norse people, regarding the creation of the world, gods, and men, and thus we find them preserved in the songs of the " Edda. The vague notion of a Deity who created and ruled over all things had its rise in the impression made upon the human mind by the unity of nature. The sun, moon, and stars, clouds and mists, storms and tempests, appeared to be higher powers, and took distinct forms in the mind of man. The sun was first regarded as a fiery bird which flew across the sky, then as a horse, and afterwards as a chariot and horses; the clouds were cows, from whose udders the fruitful rain poured down. The storm-wind appeared as a great eagle that stirred the air by the flapping of his enormous wings. These signs of nature seemed to resemble animals. On further consideration it was found that man was gifted with the higher mental powers. It was then acknowledged that the figure of an animal was an improper representation of a divine being. They thus inverted the words of Holy writ, that " God created man in his own image," and men now made the gods in their own likeness, but still regarded them as greater, more beautiful, and more ideal than themselves.

From the titles of these pagan gods we derive the names of our days of the week ,and thus we continue to perpetuate in our daily life the story of

Norse mythology. The first day of the week was dedicated to the worship of the sun. The second day to that of the moon. The third day was sacred to Tyr, the god of war. The fourth day was sacred to Wodin, or Odin, the chief deity. The fifth day was sacred to Thor, the god of thunder. The sixth day of the week, Friday, was sacred to Frigga, the wife of the great Odin. The seventh or last day of the week was dedicated by the Romans to Saturn, one of the planets, their god of agriculture, whose annual festival was a time of unrestrained enjoyment.

The "Eddas" were two Scandinavian books, the earlier a collection of mythological and heroic songs, and the other a prose composition of old and venerable traditions. These books were meant for the instruction of the Norse skalds and bards. It is believed that the learned Icelander, Saemund, the Wise, compiled the older Edda in 1056 from oral traditions, and partly from runic writings. The younger Edda is supposed to have been compiled by Bishop Snorri Sturlason in 1178, and this collection goes by the name of Snorra-Edda. The language was developed by means of the sagas and songs which had been handed down among the people from generation to generation.

The Norns were the three fatal sisters, who used to watch over the springs of water, and appeared by the cradle of many a royal infant to give it presents. On such occasions two of them were generally friendly to the child, while the third prophesied evil concerning it. In the pretty story of the "Sleeping Beauty" these Norns appear as the fairies.

Mythical Gods.

Bragi was the son of the wave maidens and the god of poetry. He was married to the blooming Induna, who accompanied him to Asgard, where she gave the gods every morning the apples of eternal youth.

Tyr, the god of war, was tall, slender as a pine, and bravely defended the gods from the terrible Fenris-Wolf. In doing so he lost his hand, and was held in high honour by the people. Baldur, the holy one, and the giver of all good, was the son of Odin. His mother Frigga entreated all creatures to spare the well-beloved, but she overlooked the weak mistletoe bough. The gods in boisterous play threw their weapons at Baldur, and the dart made of the fatal bough was thrown by the blind Hödur with deadly effect.

Forseti, the son of Baldur, resembled his father in holiness and righteousness, was the upholder of eternal law. The myth shows him seated on a throne teaching the Norsemen the benefits of the law, surrounded by his twelve judges.

Loki, the crafty god, was the father of the Fenris-Wolf, and the snake. He was the god of warmth and household fire, and was held to be the corrupter of gods, and the spirit of evil. It was Loki who formed the fatal dart, which he placed in the hands of the blind Hödur, which caused the death of Baldur. After the murder of Baldur, Loki conceals himself on a distant mountain, and hides himself under a waterfall. Here the avengers catch him in a peculiar net which he had invented for the destruction of others. They bind him to a rock, where a snake drops poison upon his face, which makes him yell with pain. His faithful wife, Sigyn, catches the poison in a cup; but still it drops upon him whenever the vessel is full. From this myth it is supposed that Shakspere derived the story of his greatest drama and tragedy, " Hamlet," of the Prince of Denmark. Our forefathers notion of the last battle, the single combats of the strong, the burning of the world, are all to be read in ancient traditions, and we find them described in the poems of the Skalds. The Norse mythology makes amends for the tragic end of the divine drama by concluding with a description of the renewal of the world. The earth rises fresh and green out of its ruin, as soon as it has been cleansed from sin, refined and restored by fire. The gods assemble on the plains of Ida, and the sons of Thor bring with them their father's storm-hammer, a weapon no longer used for fighting, but only for consecrating what is right and holy. They are joined by Baldur and Hödur, reconciled and united in brotherly love.

Uller is recorded in the Edda as the cheery and sturdy god of winter, who cared nothing for wind and snowstorm, who used to go about on long journeys on his skates or snow-shoes. These shoes were compared to a shield, and thus the shield is called Uller's Ship in many places. When the god Uller skated over the ice he carried with him his shield, and deadly arrows and bow made from the yew-tree. He lived in the Palace Ydalir, the yew vale. As he protected plants and seeds from the severe frosts of the north, by covering the ground with a coating of snow, he was regarded as the benefactor of mortal men, and was called the friend of Baldur, the giver of every blessing and joy. Uller meant divine glory, as Vulder, the Anglo-Saxon god, was also characterised. This was probably because the glory of the northern winter night, which is often brilliantly lighted by the snow, the dazzling ice, and the Aurora-borealis, the great northern light. The myths exist in the present like the stately ruins of a past time, which are no longer suitable for the use of man. Generations come and go, their views, actions, and modes of thought change:

> "All things change; they come and go;
> The pure unsullied soul alone remains in peace."

Thousands of years ago our ancestors prayed to Waruna, the father in heaven; thousands of years later the Romans entered their temple and worshipped Jupiter, the father in heaven, while the Teutonic races worshipped the All-father. After the lapse of centuries now we turn in all our sorrow and adversities to our Father which is in heaven. In the thousands of years which may pass we shall not have grown beyond this central point of religion.

> "Our little systems have their day;
> They have their day and cease to be;
> They are but broken lights of Thee,
> And Thou, O Lord, art more than they.
>
> We have but faith; we cannot know;
> For knowledge is of things we see;
> And yet we trust it comes from Thee,
> A beam in darkness, let it grow!"

In his masterly work on "Hero-Worship," Carlyle traces the growth of the "Hero as Divinity" from the Norse Mythology in the following words: "How the man Odin came to be considered a god, the chief god? His people knew no limits to their admiration of him; they had as yet no scale to measure admiration by. Fancy your own generous heart's love of some greatest man expanding till it transcended all bounds, till it filled and overflowed the whole field of your thought.

Then consider what mere Time will do in such cases; how if a man was great while living, he becomes tenfold greater when dead.

What an enormous 'camera-obscura' magnifier

is Tradition! How a thing grows in the human memory, in the human imagination, when love, worship, and all that lies in the human heart, is there to encourage it. And in the darkness, in the entire ignorance; without date or document, no book, no Arundel marble: only here and there some dumb monumental cairn. Why! in thirty or forty years, were there no books, any great man would grow 'mythic,' the contemporaries who had seen him, being once all dead: enough for us to discern far in the uttermost distance some gleam as of a small real light shining in the centre of that enormous camera-obscura image: to discern that the centre of it all was not a madness and nothing, but a sanity and something.

This light kindled in the great dark vortex of the Norse mind, dark but living, waiting only for the light, this is to me the centre of the whole. How such light will then shine out, and with wondrous thousand-fold expansion spread itself in forms and colours, depends not on *it*, so much as in the National Mind recipient of it. Who knows to what unnameable subtleties of spiritual law all these Pagan fables owe their shape! The number twelve, divisiblest of all, which could be halved, quartered, parted into three, into six, the most remarkable number, this was enough to determine the Signs of the Zodiac, the number of Odin's sons, and innumerable other twelves.

Odin's Runes are a significant feature of him.

Runes, and the miracles of "magic" he worked by them, make a great feature in tradition. Runes are the Scandinavian alphabet; suppose Odin to have been the inventor of letters as well as "magic" among that people. It is the greatest invention man has ever made, this of marking down the unseen thought that is in him by written characters. It is a kind of second speech, almost as miraculous as the first.

You remember the astonishment and incredulity of Atahaulpa the Peruvian king; how he made the Spanish soldier, who was guarding him, scratch Dios on his thumb nail, that he might try the next soldier with it, to ascertain whether such a miracle was possible. If Odin brought letters among his people, he might work magic enough! Writing by Runes has some air of being original among the Norsemen; not a Phœnician alphabet, but a Scandinavian one.

Snorro tells us farther that Odin invented poetry; the music of human speech, as well as that miraculous runic marking of it.

Transport yourself into the early childhood of nations; the first beautiful morning light of our Europe, when all yet lay in fresh young radiance, as of a great sunrise, and our Europe was first beginning to think,—to be!

This Odin, in his rude semi-articulate way, had a word to speak. A great heart laid open to take in this great universe, and man's life here, and utter a great word about it. And now, if we still admire such a man beyond all others, what must these wild Norse souls, first awakened with thinking, have made of him! The rough words he articulated, are they not the rudimental roots of those English words we still use? He worked so, in that obscure element. But he was as a light kindled in it, a light of intellect, rude nobleness of heart, the only kind of lights we have yet: he had to shine there, and make his obscure element a little lighter, as is still the task of us all.

We will fancy him to be the type Norseman; the finest Teuton whom that race had yet produced. He is as a root of many great things; the fruit of him is found growing, from deep thousands of years, over the whole field of Teutonic life. Our own Wednesday, is it not still Odin's day? Wednesbury, Wansborough, Wanstead, Wandsworth: Odin grew into England too, these are still the leaves from that root. He was the chief god to all the Teutonic peoples; their pattern Norsemen.

The essence of the Scandinavian, as indeed of all Pagan mythologies, we found to be recognition of the divineness of nature; sincere communion of man with the mysterious invisible powers, visibly seen at work in the world around him.

Sincerity is the great characteristic of it. Amid all that fantastic congeries of associations and traditions in their musical mythologies, the main practical belief a man could have was of an inflexible destiny, of the valkyrs and the hall of Odin, and that the one thing needful for a man was to be brave. The Valkyrs are choosers of the slain, who lead the brave to a heavenly hall of Odin: only the base and slavish being thrust elsewhere, into the realms of Hela, the Death goddess. This was the soul of the whole Norse Belief. Valour is still valour. The first duty of a man is still that of subduing Fear. Snorro tells us they thought it a shame and misery not to die in battle; and if a natural death seemed to be coming on, they would cut wounds in their flesh that Odin might receive them as warriors slain. Old kings about to die had their body laid into a ship, the ship sent forth with sail set and slow fire burning in it; that once out at sea, it might blaze up into flame, and in such a manner bury worthily the old hero, at once in the sky and in the ocean."

THE DESCENT OF ODIN.

(From the Norse Tongue.)

By THOMAS GRAY.

Up rose the king of men with speed,
And saddled straight his coal black steed.
Down the yawning steep he rode
That leads to Hela's drear abode.
Him the Dog of Darkness spied;
His shaggy throat he opened wide,
While from his jaws with carnage fill'd,
Foam and human gore distill'd;

Hoarse he bays with hideous din,
Eyes that glow and fangs that grin,
And long pursues with fruitless yell
The father of the powerful spell.
Onward still his way he takes,
(The groaning earth beneath him shakes)
Till full before his fearless eyes
The portals nine of Hell arise.
Right against the eastern gate
By the moss grown pile he sate,
Where long of yore to sleep was laid
The dust of the prophetic maid,
Facing to the northern clime,
Thrice he traced the Runic rhyme,
Thrice pronounced in accents dread,
The thrilling verse that wakes the dead.
Till from out the hollow ground
Slowly breathed a sullen sound.
What call unknown, what charms presume
To break the quiet of the tomb?
Who thus afflicts my troubled sprite
And drags me from the realms of night?
Long on these mouldering bones have beat
The winter's snow, the summer's heat.
The drenching dews, and driving rain,
Let me, let me sleep again.
Who is he with voice unbless'd
That calls me from the bed of rest?

Odin: A traveller to the unknown
Is he that calls; a warrior's son,
Thou the deeds of light shall know;
Tell me what is done below.
For whom yon glittering board is spread,
Dress'd for whom yon golden bed?

Proph : Mantling in the goblet see
The pure beverage of the bee,
O'er it hangs the shield of gold :
'Tis the drink of Balder bold :
Balder's head to death is given :
Pain can reach the sons of heaven !
Unwilling I my lips unclose :
Leave me, leave me to repose.

Odin : Once again my call obey ;
Prophetess ! arise and say
What dangers Odin's child await,
Who the author of his fate ?

Proph : In Hoder's hand the hero's doom ;
His brother sends him to the tomb,
Now my weary lips I close,
Leave me, leave me to repose.

Odin : Prophetess ! my spell obey ;
Once again arise and say
Who th' avenger of his guilt,
By whom shall Hoder's blood be spilt ?

Proph : In the caverns of the west,
By Odin's fierce embrace compress'd,
A wondrous boy shall rind a bear,
Who ne'er shall comb his raven hair,
Nor wash his visage in the stream,
Nor see the sun's departing beam,
Till he on Hoder's corpse shall smile,
Flaming on the funeral pile.
Now my weary lips I close,
Leave me, leave me to repose.

Odin : Yet awhile my call obey ;
Prophetess awake and say
What virgins these in speechless wo,
That bent to earth their solemn brow,

That their flaxen tresses tear,
And snowy veils that float in air?
Tell me whence their sorrows rose,
Then I leave thee to repose.

Proph: Ha! no traveller art thou:
King of Men I know thee now:
Mightiest of a mighty line.

Odin: No boding maid of skill divine,
Art thou, no prophetess of good,
But mother of a giant brood!

Proph: Hie thee hence, and boast at home,
That never shall enquirer come
To break my iron sleep again,
Till Lok his horse his tenfold chain,
Never till substantial Night,
Has re-assumed her ancient right,
Till wrapped in fumes, in ruin hurl'd,
Sinks the fabric of the world.

Superstitions

CHAPTER XIV.

SUPERSTITIONS.

The most remarkable instance of the tenacity of superstitions is the survival of the practice of "bringing in the New Year." Not only does it exist among the poor and uneducated, but even amongst educated people at this festive season. It is considered an omen of misfortune if the first person who enters your house on New Year's morning has a fair complexion or light hair. This popular prejudice has never been satisfactorily accounted for, says the late Mr. Charles Hardwick, in his "Traditions and Superstitions." He says: "I can only suggest that it most probably arose from the fact that amongst the Keltic tribes, who were the earliest immigrants, dark hair prevailed. This dark characteristic still prevails amongst the Welsh, Cornish, and Irish of the present day. When these earlier races came in contact with the Danes and Norse as enemies, they found their mortal foes to possess fair skins and light hair. They consequently regarded the intrusion into their houses, at the commencement of the year, of one of the hated race, as a sinister omen. The true Kelt does not only resent, on New Year's Day, the red hair of the Dane, but the brown and flaxen locks of the German as well." An old writer, Oliver Matthew, of Shrewsbury, writing in the year 1616, at the age of 90 years, says it was the custom of the Danes to place one of their men to live in each homestead of the conquered race, and this was more resented than the tribute they had to pay. This affords another proof that these fair-haired men were the cause of this present superstition. It is also considered unlucky to allow anything to be taken out of the house on New Year's Day, before something had been brought in. The importation of the most insignificant article, even a piece of coal, or something in the nature of food, is sufficient to prevent this misfortune, which the contrary action would render inevitable. This sentiment is well expressed in the following rhyme:—

> Take out, and then take in,
> Bad luck will begin.
> Take in, then take out,
> Good luck comes about.

It would be rash to speculate how long superstitions of this kind will continue to walk hand in hand with religion; how long traditions from far-off heathen times will exercise this spell not only in our remote country places but in enlightened towns. In the realms of folk-lore, many were firm believers in witchcraft, in signs and omens, which things were dreaded with ignorant awe, while the romantic race of gipsies look upon occult influences from the inside, as a means of personal gain.

The prophetic character of the weather during this period is a superstition common to all the Aryan tribes. So strongly is this characteristic of the season felt in Lancashire at the present day, that many country people may be met with who habitually found their "forecast" on the appearances of the heavens on Old Christmas Day. The late Mr. T. T. Wilkinson relates a singular instance of this superstition, which shows the stubbornness of traditional lore, even when subjected to the power and influence of legislative enactments. He says: "The use of the old style in effect is not yet extinct in Lancashire. The writer knows an old man of Habergham, near Burnley, about 77 years of age, who always reckons the changes of the seasons in this manner. He alleges the practice of his father and grandfather in support of his method, and states with much confidence that 'Perliment didn't change t' seasons wen they chang'd day o't' month.'" A work named "The Shepherd's Kalender," published in 1709, soberly informs us that "if New Year's Day in the morning opens with dusky red clouds, it denotes strife and debates among great ones, and many robberies to happen that year."

The Helm Wind.

In the neighbourhood of Kirkoswald, on the Eden in Cumberland, a district prolific in Arthurian legends, it is said that a " peculiar wind called the ' Helm Wind,' sometimes blows with great fury in that part of the country. It is believed by some persons to be an electrical phenomenon." This fact may have some remote connection with the superstition under consideration. Sir Walter Scott's version of the legend is as follows : "A daring horse jockey sold a black horse to a man of venerable and antique appearance, who appointed the remarkable hillock upon the Eildon Hills, called the Lucken Hare, as the place where at twelve o'clock at night he should receive the price. He came and his money was paid in ancient coin, and he was invited by his customer to view his residence. The trader in horses followed his guide in the deepest astonishment through several long ranges of stalls, in each of which a horse stood motionless, while an armed warrior lay equally still at the charger's feet. 'All these men,' said the Wizard in a whisper, ' will awaken at the battle of Sheriffmoor.' At the extremity of this extraordinary depôt hung a sword and a horn, which the Prophet pointed out to the horse dealer, as containing the means of dissolving the spell. The man in confusion, took the horn and attempted to wind it. The horses instantly started in their stalls, stamped and shook their bridles; the men arose, and clashed their armour; and the mortal terrified at the tumult he had excited, dropped the horn from his hand. A voice like that of a giant, louder even than the tumult around, pronounced these words:

> "Woe to the coward that ever he was born
> That did not draw the sword before he blew the horn!"

The mistletoe was supposed to protect the homestead from fire and other disaster, and, like other mysterious things, was believed to be potent in matters relating to courtship and matrimony. It is to this sentiment we owe the practice of kissing under the bush formed of holly and mistletoe during Christmas festivities. This matrimonial element in the mistletoe is artistically presented in the Scandinavian mythology. Freigga, the mother of Baldr, had rendered him invulnerable against all things formed out of the then presumed four elements, fire, air, earth, and water. The mistletoe was believed to grow from none of these elements. But she overlooked the one insignificant branch of the mistletoe, and it was by an arrow fashioned from it that the bright day-god Baldr, the Scandinavian counterpart of Apollo and Bel, was killed by the blind Hodr or Heldr. The gods, however, restored him to life, and dedicated the mistletoe to his mother, who is regarded as the counterpart of the classical Venus. Hence its importance in affairs of love and courtship. It is not improbable that the far-famed dart of Cupid may have some relation to the mistletoe arrow, to which the beautiful Baldr succumbed.

The medicinal qualities of the mistletoe tree were also in high repute. Its healing power was shared by the ash tree, which was the "Cloud tree" of the Norsemen. The ash (Norse "askr,") was the tree out of which the gods formed the first man, who was thence called Askr. The ash was among the Greeks, an image of the clouds, and the mother of men.

Other Christmas customs and superstitions are peculiar to Lancashire. The white thorn is supposed to possess supernatural power, and certain trees of this class, in Lancashire called Christmas thorns, are believed to blossom only on Old Christmas Day. Mr. Wilkinson says that in the neighbourhood of Burnley many people will yet travel a considerable distance "at midnight, in order to witness the blossoming." The Boar's Head yet forms a chief object amongst the dishes of Christmas festivities. Among the impersonations of natural phenomena, the wild boar represented the "ravages of the whirlwind that tore up the earth." In all mythologies the boar is the animal connected with storm and lightning. There yet exists a superstition prevalent in Lancashire to the effect that pigs can "see the wind." Dr. Kuhm says that in Westphalia this superstition is a prevalent one. The tradition is at least three or four thousand years old. Lancashire has many stories of the pranks played by the wild boar or demon pig, removing the stones in the night on the occasion of the building of churches. Stories of this nature are to be found respecting Winwick, where a rude carving resembling a hog fastened to a block of stone, by a collar, is to be seen built into the tower of the present Church. Burnley and Rochdale Churches, and Samlesbury Church, near Preston, possess similar traditions.

All Celtic nations have been accustomed to the worship of the Sun. It was a custom that everywhere prevailed in ancient times to celebrate a feast at the Winter Solstice, by which men testified their joy at seeing this great luminary return again to this part of the heavens. This was the greatest solemnity of the year. They called it in many places "Yole," or "Yuul," from the word "Hiaul" and "Houl," which even at this day signifies sun in the language of Cornwall. "Heulo" in modern Welsh means to "shine as the Sun." And thus we may derive our word halo. Some writers, including the Venerable Bede, derive Yule from "hvoel," a wheel, meaning the return of the Sun's annual course after the Winter Solstice.

Agriculture

A COMPARISON OF PROGRESS BETWEEN DANISH AND BRITISH

CHAPTER XV.

Agriculture.

While the Scandinavian element is regarded by modern writers as the predominating feature in the composition of Englishmen, the Danish has been the pre-eminent force in forming the character of the race which dominates the Lancashire people of to-day. In our survey of the progress of the race, from the earliest settlement of the Danes, we find the impression of their footprints in the place-names of the county, which are our oldest and most enduring monuments. Following their character of daring and venture, we have established a maritime power which is the envy of the world. The same spirit which formed our early settlements in Lancashire has founded colonies in every quarter of the globe. The enterprise of the early "copemen" has developed into our mercantile fleet, which controls the carrying trade of the seas. The voice of their language still resounds in the names of our laws, the "hundreds" of the county, and in our system of administration, and also in the political freedom which has established the saying that "What Lancashire says to-day, England will say to-morrow."

In the earliest record of agricultural progress we find the Danes have given us the name of "husbandry," and the modern implement called the "plough." Therefore, in forming an estimate of the benefits which have resulted from our intercourse with the Danes, the primary industry of agriculture and dairy produce must not be omitted. In all other branches of commercial activity, by the application of scientific methods, unbounded progress has been achieved. Has the oldest industry of the county had a share in this attainment of wealth, or its rural population derived advancement? For a period of half-a-century our agricultural leaders have held competitions known as agricultural shows, where valuable prizes have been given for live stock of all descriptions, and rewards for every design of mechanical appliance for agriculture. To a stranger visiting these shows, it would appear that we brooked no rival in the production of dairy produce. What are the facts disclosed by the figures for the past 25 or 50 years? In the "Year Book of the Lancashire Past Agricultural Students' Association" we are told that Parliament handed over, in the year 1890, to local authorities, large sums of money for purposes of technical instruction, and that "this marks the really substantial beginning of agricultural education in Lancashire."

With this statement, made at the opening of the twentieth century, it may be interesting to notice the increase of our imports of Danish dairy produce for a period of eleven years:—

Year.	Imports.	Exports.
1897	£10,968,397	£3,476,663
1898	£11,703,384	£3,919,326
1899	£12,432,977	£4,399,025
1900	£13,187,667	£4,724,181
1901	£14,234,102	£4,163,478
1902	£15,556,780	£4,033,897
1903	£16,594,565	£4,398,088
1904	£15,911,615	£3,925,836
1905	£15,416,456	£4,476,624
1906	£16,433,648	£5,162,428
1907	£18,262,542	£6,124,039

Danish Agriculture.

During the past ten years, says Mr. Consul L. C. Liddell in his report for 1908, Denmark has witnessed a considerable increase.

The exports of agricultural produce, which in 1904 were worth £18,400,000, reached £22,400,000 in 1908. The amount of butter exported to the United Kingdom reaches 96.1 per cent. of the total; of bacon, 97.5 per cent.; and of eggs, 98.8 per cent. The remainder of the butter and bacon goes principally to Germany. Nearly the entire export of horses and cattle is absorbed by the German market, whilst three-fifths of the beef also finds its way thither, the remainder going to Norway.

The labour question has, as in other years, attracted much attention. The number of Swedish and Finnish labourers is decreasing, and it is from Galicia that Denmark would now appear to recruit her farm hands. The number of Galician "season" labourers in 1908 reached 8,000, or about 1,000 more than in 1907. The co-operative organisations approached the Prime Minister with the proposal that free passes should be granted on the State railway system to any unemployed at Copenhagen having a knowledge of field work to help in farming. This attempt to organise a "back to the land" movement is not expected to be attended with success.

These figures show an increase of nearly double in eleven years, or an increase of eight millions, and an increase of two millions from 1906 to 1907.

It must be remembered that the bulk of Danish produce comes to the Manchester market, and is distributed from that centre. An analysis of the 1907 imports from Denmark gives the following details:—Butter £10,192,587, eggs £1,774,319, fish £91,031, lard £17,723, bacon £5,385,275, pork £200,000. The item of bacon for 1907 shows an increase of one million pounds over the year 1906.

The import of Danish produce began in the early sixties of last century, and the quality was so indifferent that we are told it was fortunate if two casks of butter were good out of every five. Even then the quality was superior to Irish butter in its taste and appearance. The population of Denmark is two and a half millions, and the cultivated area of land is seven million acres. The yield of crops to the acre is 28 bushels of wheat, while in England it is 33 bushels. In barley the yield is 30 bushels to our 35 bushels, and in oats it is 33 bushels to our 42. These figures show the comparative fruitfulness of the land to be in favour of England. The live stock per 1,000 population in Denmark is 711 cattle to our 267, and pigs 563 to our 82. The total imports for twenty years show that our dairy produce from abroad has doubled, and is increasing at a rapid rate.

Comparisons of Danish methods of farming to-day cannot be made with the present conditions existing in Lancashire or Yorkshire, but can only be made by the modern conditions now obtaining in Essex under Lord Rayleigh.

Crops Diminishing.

What has been the course of our agriculture for the past sixty years? Mr. Cobden maintained that Free Trade would do no injury to agriculture. The following is a comparison of prices in the years 1845 and 1907:—

	1845.		1907.
*4lbs. loaf of Bread	6d.	......	5½d.
†1lb. Butter	7d.	......	1/1.
†1lb. Cheese	2d.	......	9d.
†1lb. Bacon	3d.	......	9d.
†1lb. Beef	4d.	......	8d.

* From "Free Trader," issued by the Liberal Free Traders, Dec., 1904.
† From "The Hungry Forties," written by Mr. Cobden's daughter.

Sixty years ago home-grown wheat produced flour for twenty-four millions of our population.* To-day it produces flour for four and a half millions. The acreage under wheat has been reduced in the last thirty years to one-half in England, to one-third in Scotland, and to one-fifth in Ireland. The same is true of green crops. Nine hundred thousand acres less are under crops than were thirty years ago. The same may be said of the area under hop cultivation, which has been reduced every year. The only bright spot in the review of our agricultural position, extending over many years, is to be found in the growth of fruit, although this has not increased as rapidly as foreign importations.

The result of these changes during the yast thirty years has been an increase of imports of agricultural produce of eighty millions. Our imports of wheat have increased by thirty-two millions, our imports of dairy produce have increased by twenty-one millions, and eggs alone have increased by four millions sterling a year; while fruit and vegetables have increased by ten and a half millions. The effect of this must be the increased dependence of our population on foreign supplies. Agriculture finds employment for a million less than it did sixty years ago. These are facts and not opinions, and we are compelled to use the figures of the general national imports, as the details of the counties are not available.

* From Report of Agricultural Committee of the Tariff Commission.

National Savings.

Statesmen tell us that the Post Office Savings Bank deposits are a fair indication of the industrial prosperity. In the report of these Post Office Savings Banks we find that Denmark heads the list with £15 11s. per head of the population, while the United Kingdom comes ninth in the list with a sum of £4 11s. per head of the population.

The economy of waste has been the keynote of wealth to many industries, and the adaptability of labour to changed conditions has marked the survival of more than one centre of commercial activity. Individual cases are not wanting to prove that men who have been found unfit to follow their work in mills and town employments through weak health or the effect of accidents, have succeeded, by the aid of a small capital, in becoming model farmers, and have demonstrated the variety of crops and stock which can be raised on a single farm. The bye-products of the manufacturers are often the source of success, and these are the most neglected in the itinerary of the farmer.

The greatest problem which confronts our municipal authorities is the profitable disposal of sewage. Where sewage farms are maintained they are invariably conducted at a heavy loss to the ratepayers, while the adjoining farm tenants often succeed in making profits. To reclaim the land which has gone out of cultivation, by the application of unemployed labour and the disposal of waste and sewage, provides the solution of a difficulty which may become a source of wealth, and restore the prosperity of a lost industry.

Cost of Agricultural Education.

A White paper just issued by the Board of Education gives particulars as to the amount spent by County Councils in England and Wales on agricultural education.

The amounts vary considerably in the different counties for the year ending March, 1908. In England, Lancashire takes the lead with £7,485, and in Wales the county of Carmarthen is prominent with £597.

The gross total amounted to £79,915, of which £21,662 was in grants to schools and colleges, £9,876 for scholarships, and £12,433 for dairy instruction.

The figures are approximate owing to the difficulty of analysing education accounts.

There are not wanting those who say that farming cannot be made to pay in England. Essex has quite a different experience. For here farms, varying in size from 250 acres to 5,000 and over, have been made to return very good profits. The whole secret lies in the work being conducted on scientific principles, and the careful watching of every penny expended, as well as giving the labourers a direct interest in getting good results.

On Lord Rayleigh's estate, Terling, which comprises about 5,000 acres, striking results have been obtained during the past twenty years, his successes being attributed to the use of business and scientific methods. For many years past his lordship's brother, the Hon. E. G. Strutt—probably one of the most experienced practical farmers in England—has had the management of the property, and has shown that farming can be carried on with a profit in this country.

Essex is described as flat, but in the neighbourhood of Terling, which abuts on the Great Eastern Railway line at Witham, there are numerous gently undulating plains, and even at this time of the year a stroll along the lanes in the neighbourhood reveals many pleasant surprises. Here and there the hedgerows are already bursting into delicate green buds, and in some places the crops sown during the early winter for spring are showing above the rich dark brow soil. And many are the birds which are already, as it were, getting into voice for the spring. The county hereabouts is heavily wooded, the chief trees being oak, ash, and elm. Many of these are veritable giants and monarchs of the forest, now standing out alone on the sky-line in all their nakedness of winter outline, then in small groups, again in such numbers as to become forests. On every hand are signs of activity. Ploughing for the moment is all over, though there are still fields of stubble which have to be turned over and prepared for crops in the near future. Fields which have already been ploughed are being heavily manured in readiness for sowing. And herein lies one of the secrets of the successful farming prevailing in this favoured neighbourhood. Everyone knows, but not everyone acts upon the knowledge, that as the fertility of the soil is exhausted fresh nutriment must be given. The observance of this rule brings its own reward, as many have learned to their advantage. Hedging and ditching are in progress, and by the time that all hands will be required on the land for ploughing, scarifying, harrowing, and sowing, hedges will have been trimmed and ditches cleaned.

Some eighteen or twenty years ago Lord Rayleigh decided to offer all his farm labourers, who number about 250, bonuses on the profits of their industry. This scheme proved eminently successful; so much so, indeed, that Lord Rayleigh has now gone a step further and offered to give every man who cares to invest his savings in his farms 4 per cent. interest on such money, and a share in any profits which may accrue after that dividend has been paid. A very large proportion of the men employed have taken advantage of this offer, which gives them close upon 2 per cent. more than they were getting from the Post Office Savings Bank, where they had been in the habit of putting their money, for they are a thoroughly respectable, self-respecting, and frugal community. It is now just a year since this offer was first made, and the employees put up over £1,000, in sums ranging from £1 to £100, the latter sum coming from a man who had banked all the bonuses he earned, along with savings from twenty-five years' earnings.

Lord Rayleigh's idea was to get the men not only to study thrift, but to take a keener interest in their daily work. It has been said that that man is a public benefactor who gets two blades of grass to flourish where but one grew before. His lordship has a far higher satisfaction in advancing the position of the men in his employment. In effect this is what he said to them: "My farms represent so much money to me; now for every £1 which you put in I will guarantee you 4 per cent. After we have all had our 4 per cent., such surplus profit as may be left, if any, will be divided between us *pro rata*." The result of the first year's farming under this form of co-partnership has been very satisfactory. Everyone has not only been paid the guaranteed 4 per cent., which was distributed recently, but each labourer has also received a share in the sum which was over after paying out that amount. While Mr. Strutt declined to disclose the exact amount of the remaining profit, he hinted that the extra interest might quite possibly be as much as a further 4 per cent. Whatever it is, every labourer who put his savings into Lord Rayleigh's hands is congratulating himself upon his good fortune, and, as saving begets saving, there is a prospect that none of these beneficiaries will ever need the old age pension.

Lord Rayleigh has made only two stipulations with his men, both aimed at unity of administration. One is that they cannot have any voice in the management of the estate, which Mr. Strutt naturally works to the best advantage, and the other is that only the savings of the labourer himself and his wife may be offered for investment in the farms.

Probably there is no farm where such intricate or such useful books are kept as on the Terling estates. Practically every field is treated as a separate farm in itself. Say, for instance, a field is to be sown with wheat. It has to be ploughed, the cost of which is charged in the book against that field, as also the value of the manure used, the price of the seeds sown, and all the time occupied in preparing the land, and, later on, in cutting the wheat, threshing, and sending it to market. On the opposite page of the ledger is put the amount obtained for the grain, and the value of the straw, whether sold or used on the farms. A balance can then be struck, and the profit or loss shown at a glance. On the profit shown, those who did the various necessary labours receive their bonus. So with every field. But the system does not end here. A most careful record is kept, for example, of every cow—the original cost, if bought, the amount of milk she yields per year, of her calves, and what they fetch when sold, or their value if retained on the estate. Every Friday, the morning and evening milkings are accurately measured, and at the end of the year these figures are added up and multiplied by seven for the seven days of the week. In this way it is known exactly how much milk each cow gives. The annual average should be about 800 gallons, which is regarded as a very fair amount. There is, however, one cow, Lilac by name, which seems to despise that average. Last year her yield of milk was no less than 1,457 gallons, which is a big record, even on the Terling estates.

Mr. Strutt reckons that a cow should give on an average 650 gallons of milk per year, and the cowmen get a bonus when the yield of the cows in their charge average that amount. The advantage of such records are enormous. If a cow does not give 650 gallons of milk per annum, she is at once sold, as she does not pay for her keep. As there are no less than 800 cows on the estate, the keeping of such records involves an enormous amount of work, but it is work which has a profitable result, facilitating, as it does, the weeding out of poor dairy stock.

The same attention is paid to other departments. Records are kept of the sheep, of which there are considerable flocks scattered over the fifteen farms comprised in the estate. It is the same with poultry, of which there are thousands roaming about the farms, grubbing much of their food, but, of course, some is thrown down for them in the various poultry yards. No hens are penned up on the estate. While that course is necessary where prize-show birds are reared, in the case of table poultry and poultry kept for eggs pens are neither essential nor profitable. With freedom the birds lay more regularly, and are generally in better condition for the table.

Asked as to whether eggs were not lost owing to the hens laying in the hedges, Mr. Isted, who is in charge of the office where all the various books of record are kept, said that few, indeed, if any, are overlooked by those responsible, because of the system of bonuses given by Lord Rayleigh, to which reference has already been made. Those in charge of the hens receive a reward on every score of eggs brought in. Every head of poultry reared also means a monetary benefit to the workers.

Daily between 60 and 80 17-gallon churns of milk are despatched to London. It is said that from no station along the Great Eastern Railway line is more milk sent to the Metropolis than from Witham. At present about 100 of these churns leave the station every day, all the milk coming from the immediate neighbourhood. Eggs are also sent to the Rayleigh Dairies in vast quantities. Every egg is carefully tested before it leaves the estate. The poultry is disposed of through middlemen. Other produce is sold in the Essex markets—at Chelmsford, Colchester, Witham, and Braintree. This would include all the cereals not used on the farm, and such hay as was not required for the stock during winter.

Down in Essex wages are regarded as generally good by the farm labourers. At least there is a distinct tendency on the part of the men to remain on the soil. Horsemen receive 14s. a week, cowmen 14s. and 15s., the head cowmen getting generally 18s. and 20s., while other farm hands earn from 13s. to 15s. Living is very cheap, and rents are low. A good, comfortable cottage, with a decent bit of garden, where vegetables can be grown, can be had for £4 or £5 a year. Should a man require more ground he can get it at a nominal annual rent of 3d. per rod—that is, a piece of ground measuring 5½ yards each way. Quite a number of men avail themselves of this offer, and as they knock off work at five p.m., they put in their evenings on their own "estate."

It is true that Lord Rayleigh has only tried his new system of investment, as well as interest in the farms, for a year, but the results amply justify the experiment. So satisfied are the men themselves that many have asked to be allowed to invest their share of the interest earned and their new bonuses in the estate. It would seem that here, at least, is a possible project for checking the ever-increasing rush of young men to the towns, where, while wages may be higher, the conditions are not conducive to either personal or patriotic well-being. The great feature of Lord Rayleigh's plan is that it is a distinctly profit-sharing one, for no reform, however attractive, can be economically good unless it is financially sound.

With wheat in a rising market at 50s. a quarter, the granaries of the world holding back supplies a considerable proportion of which are already cornered in America—and bread dearer than it has been for many years, the question of the moment is, Can England become her own wheat grower?

Fourteen weeks after harvest the home supplies are exhausted. Britain needs altogether, both home and foreign, 30,000,000 quarters of wheat per annum to provide her people with bread. Out of the total area of 32,000,000 acres under crops of all sorts in the country only 1,625,000 acres are devoted to the growth of wheat. English climatic conditions can be relied upon to allow an average production of three and a half quarters per acre.

The solution of the problem, therefore, is simplicity itself. A matter of 8,000,000 acres taken from those devoted meantime to other crops, to pasturage (to say nothing of deer forests, grouse moors, golf links), or even lying waste, and developed for wheat growing would produce, roughly speaking, the extra 28,000,000 necessary to our annual national food supply.

Millions of acres of the land at present in other crops has grown wheat at a profit in the past. In the sixties and seventies the staple commodity was at its most remunerative price. In 1867 it touched the enormous average of 64s. 5d. per quarter, while later, in 1871 and 1873, it stood at 56s. 8d. and 58s. 8d. per quarter.

With the countries of the East—India, China, Japan—awakening to the potentialities of wheat as a food in place of rice, with America's prairies becoming used up and her teeming millions multiplying, and with Canada, Australia, and Argentina remaining at a standstill as regards wheat production, it is clear that England ought to become self-sufficing

To attain the desired end the vast possibilities of the agricultural science of to-day must be appreciated and developed by every possible means.

What can be done within England's own borders is the chief point to be considered, and some experiments and experiences may point the way.

The first question is, would home produced wheat pay? Farmers tell us that at 30s. a quarter wheat is just worth growing, but that each shilling over 30s. means about 5s. clear profit. Would not wheat at 40s. an acre be worth cultivating?

As to the practical ways and means of obtaining this sum out of the soil, I must detail some of the more modern scientific methods in agriculture.

I have said that 8,000,000 acres of the present area under crops could make us independent of foreign supplies. By applying certain simple rules of selection regarding seeds, a much smaller area of land would give the same result.

Instead of $3\frac{1}{2}$ quarters per acre—the present average—the yield could be doubled, or even trebled. Thirty years ago, in France, three quarters an acre was considered a good crop, but the same soil with improved methods of cultivation nowadays yields at least four quarters per acre; while in the best soils the crop is only considered good when it yields five quarters to six quarters an acre.

The work of the Garton brothers and of Professor Biffen, of Cambridge University, has clearly shown that by careful selection and crossing of the best breeds of wheat the yield can be actually quadrupled.

Hallet's famous experiments in selection demonstrate that the length of the wheat ear can be doubled, and the number of ears per stalk nearly trebled. The finest ear he developed produced 123 grains, as against 47 in the original ear, and 52 ears to one plant, as against ten in the original.

In agriculture, as in other matters in which England claims to take a leading part, we have something to learn from the Continent. France, Belgium, and Germany have adopted a system of co-operation which has reduced the cost of farming to the smallest possible limit. From a fund supplied partly by the Governments of these countries and partly by the farmers themselves, small farms, manures, seeds, machinery, etc., are provided on a co-operative basis. Would not a system on similar lines have far-reaching results in this country?

Perhaps the most interesting suggestion, the newest in the fields of scientific agriculture research, is the inoculation of the soil with bacteria. Through these wonder-working germs which live in the nodules of plant roots multiplication of the free nitrogen in the air goes on with great rapidity, and this, united with other elements, forms valuable plant food.

Recent experiments, the results of which have not yet been made public, show that good crops of wheat may be grown in the poorest soil; indeed, the Scriptural injunction about sowing seeds in waste places no longer bears scientific examination. On an area which was little more than common sand crops inoculated with bacteria gave an increased yield of 18 per cent.

Wheat grown on the lines I have touched upon within the United Kingdom, and paying the grower 40s. per quarter, would go far to solve every social and economic problem known. There would be work for all in the country districts, and consequently less poverty in the towns, and to the nation's resources would be conserved the enormous annual expenditure on foreign wheat of £67,000,000.

Occupying Ownership.

" A time there was, ere England's griefs began,
When every rood of ground maintained its man,"
Behold a change; where'er her flag unfurled,
It presaged forth—goods-maker to the world.
Then wealth from trade, pure farming handicapped
While glittering towns the youthful swain entrapped.
In trade, no longer, England stands alone,
Indeed, too oft, John Bull gets "beaten on his own."
Dependent on the world for nearly every crumb,
Is this a time when patriots should be dumb?
For England needs to guard 'gainst future strife
That backing up which comes from rural life.
Though all indeed may use both book and pen,
The nation's weal depends on robust men
Inured to toil—a hardy, virile band.
And these are bred where owners till the land.

Supply of Wheat.

Strides in the Scale of Living.

Earl Carrington, President of the Board of Agriculture, presided at a meeting of the Society of Arts, when a paper upon the production of wheat was read by Mr. A. E. Humphries. His lordship gave some very interesting jottings from family history, showing the great advance that had taken place in the scale of living. The subject of the lecture, he said, reminded him that over 100 years ago his grandfather, who was President of the Board of Agriculture, made a speech in which he said that one of the most important subjects with which the Board had to deal was the scarcity of wheat. It was curious that they were discussing the same subject to-day. His father, who was born 103 years ago, had often told him that in the early part of last century they did not have white bread at every meal, as it was so scarce. If that happened at the table of old Robert Smith, the banker, at Whitehall, what must the bread of the working classes have been like!

In the five years from 1878 to 1882, said Mr. Humphries in his lecture, we produced 117 lb. of wheat per head per annum, and imported 238 lb., while in the years from 1903 to 1907 we produced only 68 lb. per head, and imported 284 lb. For many years British wheat had been sold at substantially lower prices than the best foreign, and in the capacity of making large, shapely, well-aerated and digestible loaves the home-grown grain was notably deficient. It was commonly attributed to our climate, and people said that Great Britain was not a wheat producing country. The real reason was that farmer did not grow the right kind of wheat. It was not a matter of climate or of soil, but of of catering for the particular kind of soil in which the grain was to be grown. The crux of the whole question was to obtain a variety of seed that would suit the environment. Farmers, instead of aiming at quality, had striven to get as large a yield per acre as possible.

The Hon. J. W. Taverner, Agent-General for Victoria, said that he had heard a lot of talk about the efficiency of the Territorial Army and the safety of the country. If only the men were fed on bread baked from Australian wheat England had nothing to fear, for the men would be equal to anything.

Index

INDEX

Acle, 28.
Adamson, 63.
Adalis, 32, 38, 39.
Aella, King, 24.
Agriculture, 215.
Ainsdale, 7.
Aire, 159.
Ale, 16.
Alexandria, 152.
Alfred the Great (illust.), 26, 33.
Altcar, 23.
Amleth, 173.
Alfgier, 38–39.
Amounderness, 5.
Anastasius, 68.
Anderson, 63.
Angel choir of Lincoln, 170.
Anglian population, 17.
Anlaby, 13.
Anlaf, 25, 32, 35, 36, 37, 41.
Anstice, 68.
Aradr, 112.
Aratum, 112.
Arcle, 28.
Arnside Knott, 48.
Arncliffe, 27.
Art, 174.
Athelfloed, Lady of the Mercians, 104.
Athelstan, 26, 30, 33, 34, 35, 37, 49.
Asia, 158.
Augustin, 68.
Austin, 68.
Austria, 158.
Australia, 158.
Axle, 28.
Ayton (great), 27.
Back o'th' hill, 40.
Bacup, 34.
Balder, 62.
Ball (Olaf), 53.
Ballads and War Songs, 172.
Ballr, 53.
Balderstone, 62.
Bamber, 84.
Banbury, 31.
Bannister, 68.
Barrowford, 32.
Barker, 68.
Basket making, 140.
Bath-day, 15.
Battlefield, 37.
Battlestone, 37.
Beckett, 69.
Beck, 69.
Bede, 49.
Beer, 16.
Bellum brun, 35.
Bernicia, 24, 25, 50.
Bessingby, 18.
Billingr, 62.
Birkdale, 7.
Birket, 22.
Bishop's leap, 31, 35.
Bishop's House Estate, 37.
Blagburnshire hundred, 5.
'Blakogr,' 28.
Blawith, 28.
Blowick, 28.
'Boer,' 84.
'Bois,' 69.
'Bondr,' 24.
Bonfire hill, 40.

Booth, 84.
Boulsworth, 32.
Boys, 69.
Bractaetes, 174.
'Breck,' 67.
Bridlington, 18.
Britons, 1.
—— of Strathclyde, 34.
Broadclough Dykes, 41.
Broad Dyke, 34.
Broadbank, 35.
Brock, 69.
Brincaburh, 30.
Brinkburn, 30.
Bromborough, 31.
Brownedge, 35, 40.
Brownend, 40.
Brownside, 35.
Brun, 28, 29.
Brunanburh, 28, 31.
Brunford, 30.
Brunton, 31.
Brumbridge, 30.
Brumby, 31.
'Bud,' 84.
'Burh,' 31.
Burnley, 29, 48.
Burscough, 23.
Buerton, 84.
Burton, 84.
Burton-on-Trent, 24.
Bushel-corn, 99.
'By-law,' 8.
'Byr,' 84.
Byrom, 84.
Byzantine Coins, 174.

Cairns, 185.
Calday, 22.
Calders, 22.
Calderstones, 22, 182.
Canute, 5, 177.
Candlemas, 155.
Capenhurst, 64.
Castle hill—Tunlay, 33-34.
Cat's cradle, 158.
Causeway, 33.
Carnaby, 18.
Castercliffe, 32, 35.
Celtic burial, 185.
Chapman, 64.
Cheap, 64.
Cheapside, 64.
Chepstow, 64.
Chester, 4, 23, 163–164.
Chester-le-street, 53.
Children's games, 158.
Childwall, 23.
Christian 'Sunday Letters,' 153.
Churches, 163–164.
Churchtown, 164.
Claughton-on-brock, 124.
Clitheroe, 32, 48.
Clog almanacs, 143.
—— —— symbols, 144.
Coinage, 175.
Colne, 32.
Constantine, King of Scots, 30.
Copeman, 64.
Copeland, 64.
Copenhagen, 64.
Copley, 64.
Copethorn, 64.
Copynook, 34.
Corn spirit, 158.
Cottingham, 13.
Craik, Yorkshire, 51.
Crathorne, 26.
Crosby, 6, 23.
Crosses, 195.
Croxteth, 19.
Cuerdale, 7, 28, 175.
Cumberland, 53.
Cuthbert, Saint, 50, 53.
Cutherd, Bishop, 53.
Cup-cuttings, 182.

'Dale,' 7.
Danelag, 8.
Danes house, 41.
Darvel cakes, 66.
Darvel deathfeast, 66.
Dean, 69.
Deira, 9, 11, 12, 24.
Dell, 69.
Derby, 5.
Dialect, 69.
Drengs, 24.

Eadred, Abbot of Carlisle, 50.
Eanfrid, 25.
Easden Fort, 34.
Easington, 26.
Ecclesiologist, 156.
Ecfrith, 25.
Edward the Elder, 34.
Edwin, King, 24.
Egbert (illust.), 33.
Eglis, 39.
Egyptian scholars, 152.
Ellerburn, 27.
Elston, 62.
Elswick, 62.
Emmott, 41.
Enderby, 84.
Endrod, 84.
'Endr,' 84.
Entwistle, 84.
Equinox, vernal, 152.
Ernot, 35.
Everett, 68.
Everard, 68.
Extwistle Hall, 35.

Facid, 84.
Facit, 84.
Fairs and Wakes, 65.
Fawcett, 84.
'Feldkirk,' 31.
Fire and sun worship, 154.
Folklore for children, 157.
Formby, 6, 23.
Forseti, 84.
Foster, 84.
Fraisthorpe, 62.
Frankby, 62.
Fraser, 62.
Freyer, 62.
Frisby, 62.
Fry, 62.
Fryer, 62.
Furness, 164.
Fylde, 5.

'Gaard,' 75.
Gamelson, 84.
Gambleside, 84.
Gamul, 84.
'Gata,' 54.
Galt, 65.
Garnett, 68.
Garth, 75.
Garton, 75.
Garstang, 75.
Garswood, 75.
Geld, 65.
Godley, 32, 33.
Golden numbers, 144.
'Gos,' 69.
Gosford, 69.
Grave mounds, 184.
Grindalbythe, 18.
Guthred, King, 51, 52.

Hackenhurst, 39.
Haggate, 36.
Halfdene, 13, 15, 26.
Halfdan's death, 51.
Halton, 121, 125, 177–179.
—— Crosses, 179.
—— Torque, 177.
Hamilton Hill, 36, 40.
Hamlet, 173.

Hapton, 48.
Harbreck, 19.
Harkirke, 7, 177.
'Haugr,' 6.
Hay, 55.
Haydon Bridge, 51.
Hazel Edge, 36.
Hell Clough, 40.
Helm Wind, 208.
Heptarchy, 25.
Heriot, 107.
Hessle, 18.
Heysham, 121.
Highlawhill, 36.
'Hofs,' 6.
Horelaw pastures, 36.
'Hlith,' 48.
Hoe, 112.
Hogback stone, 105, 121, 179.
Hoop, 48.
Hope, 48.
Hopehead, 48.
Hopeton, 48.
Hopekirk, 48.
Hoylake, 55.
Howick, 55.
Hudleston, 96.
Hundred Court, 14.
Hutton John, 96.
Hurstwood, 35.
Husbandry, 111, 112.
Hustings, 8.
Huyton, 55.
Hyngr, the Dane, 37, 38.

Ida, King, 24.
Ingleby, 50.
Invasion and Conquest, 1, 2, 3.
Irby, 22.
Ireland, 180.
Irish Christians, 180.
Ivar, 22.

Jarls, 49.
Jarrow, 26.

Kell, 65.
Kellet, 65.
Kendal, 164.
Kingo, poet, 170.
Kirk Ella, 17, 18.
Kirk Levington, 27.
Kirkby, 6, 18.
Kirkby in Cleveland, 27.
Kirkby Moorside, 27, 164.
Kirkby Misperton, 27.
Kirkby Stephen, 164.
Kirkby Lonsdale, 164.
Kirkdale, 5, 6, 19, 27.
'Kirkja' Church, 6.
'Knotta,' 48.
Knott End Mill, 48.
Knottingley, 48.
Knut, 48.
'Knutr,' 48.
Knutsford, 48.

'Lake,' game, 157.
Land Tenure, 90.
Laugardag, bath day, 15.
Lawmen, 23.
Lay of Norse gods, 173.
Loom, Danish, 80.
Lorton-en-le-Morthen, Yorks., 33.
Leamington, 84.
Lethbridge, 48.
Levishan, 27.
Lindsey, 65.
Lindisfarne, 25.
Litherland, 48.
Literature, 168.
—— 'skryke of day,' 170.
—— sunrise, 170.
Lithgoe, 48.
Lithe, 48.

Liverpool, 23, 47.
Log-law, 81.
Long hundred, 13.
Long weight, 13.
Lonsdale, 4.
Lorton, 51.
'Lug-mark,' 81.
Lunar cycle, 155.
Lund, 65.
Lyster, 65.

Mackerfield, 54.
Maeshir, 54.
Maiden Way, 51.
Manchester, 34.
Manorial exaction, 106.
Manx Inscriptions, 138.
Memorials, 161.
Mercia, 25.
Mercians, Lady of, 34.
—— rule, 24.
'Merchet,' 106.
Mereclough, 39.
Mersey, 34.
'Messe staves,' 142.
Moons, changes, 143.
Mythology, 189.

Names, Norse and Anglo Saxon, 113.
Nelson, Admiral, 56.
Neilson, 56.
Norns, 189.
Norse Festival, 55.
Northumbria, 25, 27, 70.
Northumberland, —.
Nunnington, 23, 27.

'Occupying ownership,' 234.
Odin, 6, 197.
—— 'The descent of,' 199.
'Ol,' 16.
'Oller,' 62.
Olave, Saint, 63.
'Oter,' 63.
Otter, 63.
Ottley, 63.
Oram, 63.
'Orm,' 63.
Orme, 63.
Ormerod, 63.
Ormesby, 27.
Ormeshaw, 63.
Ormside cup, 131.
Ormskirk, 23, 63.
Ormstead, 185.
Osmotherley, 27.
'Osric,' 25.
'Oswald,' 25.
'Oxl,' 28.
Oxton, 22.

Paton, 85.
Patronymics, 60.
'Pecthun,' 85.
Penda, 25.
Peyton, 85.
Physical types, 79.
Picton, 85.
Picts, 85, 115.
Picture, 85.
Piko, 115.
Place names, 14–47.
Plough, 112.
'Plogr. plov.,' 112.
Political Freemen, 89.
Phauranoth, 152.
Preston, 23.
Prestune, 23.
Prim-staves, 142.
Prima-luna, 142.

Quakers, 99.

Raby, 22.
Rachdam, 84.
Ragnvald, 52.

Raven, 115.
Ravenshore, 115.
Ravensmeols, 23.
Rawtenstall, 48.
Red-Lees, 33–36.
Regnold of Bamborough, 34.
Ribble, 29–34.
'Ridings,' Yorkshire, 9.
Rimstock, 143–144.
'Rimur,' 143.
Rivington Pike, 115.
Roby, 23.
Rochdale, 84.
Roman days, 26.
Rooley, 39.
Rossendale, 84.
Round Hill, 40.
Royal Charters, Norse witnesses, 15.
Rûnâ, 137.
Runes, 137.
Runic Almanacs, 141.
—— Calender, 155.
—— Characters, 143, 153.
—— Inscriptions, 138.
—— 'Futhork,' 139.
—— Monuments, 181.
'Ruthlie,' 39.

'Saetter,' 22.
Sagas, 169, 174.
Salford hundred, 5.
Satterthwaite, 22.
Saxifield, 30, 35, 42.
Scarisbrick, 67.
Seacombe, 22.
Sellafield, 22.
Seascale, 22.
Seathwaithe, 22.
Settlements, 12.
'Servi,' 103.
Sherborne, 37.
Sheffield, 35.
Shotwick, 17.
Sieward, Earl, 163.
Shakespere, 193.
Skelmersdale, 78.
Skelton, 27.
Skidby, 18.
Skipper, 55.
Sigurd-Story, 179.
Sinnington, 23.
'Sinfin,' 39, 40.
'Sithric,' King, 35.
'Socage,' 16, 20, 21.
Sochmanni, 19, 91.
Sochman, 14, 20.
Sochmanries, 20.
Socmen of Peterboro', 105.
Sodor and Man, 83.
Speke, 66.
Solar cycle, 155.
'Spika,' 65.
Statesmen, 104.
Stainton, 26–7.
Steadsmen, 104.
Stokesley, 26.
Stigand, 68.
Stiggins, 68.
Stone Crosses, 119.
Storeton, 22.
Slavery abolition, 103.
'Stockstede,' Croxteth, 23.
Sudreyjar, 83.
Superstitions, 159, 205.
Sun, 152.
Sutherland, 83.
Swarbrick, 67.
Sweden 'lake' game, 156.
Swindene, 40.
S'winless lane, 35, 37.
S'winden water, 37.

Tacitus, historian, 138.
'Tallage,' 107.
Tanshelf, Taddnesscylfe, 28.
Thane, 16.

Thinghow, 28, 50.
Thingstead, 28.
'Thing,' trithing, 8.
Thingwall, 8, 13, 28, 50.
Thorold, 38.
Thorolf, 38.
Thornaby, 27.
'Thor,' 62.
Thorley, 62.
Thelwall, 23, 34.
Thurston water, 38.
Thursby, 62.
Tingley, 28, 50.
Torque, 177.
Towneley, 33.
Towthorp, 18.
Toxteth, 23.
Trawden, 48.
Troughton, 48.
Troughton, 48.
Trowbridge, 48.
'Trow'-trough, 48.
Tree-yggdrasil, 180.
'Trithing,' 7, 10.
Trithing Court, 14.
Thurstaston, 62.
Turketul, Chancellor, 39.
Turton, 62.
Tursdale, 62.
Twist hill, 40.
Tynwald, 8.

Ullersthorpe, 62.
Ullscarth, 28.
Ullswater, 28.
Ulpha, 23.
Ulverston, 62.
Unthank, 22.

Valour, 199.
Valkyrs, 199.
'Vë,' 62.
Verstigan, 143.
'Viborg,' 62.
Viking age, 178.

Wallhalla, 189.
Walton le dale, 5.
Watling street, 33.
Walkyries, 189.
Wallasey, 22.
Walshaw, 33.
Wandsworth, 198.
Wansborough, 198.
Wanstead, 198.
Wapentake, 8–9.
Warcock-hill, 36.
Warcock, 28.
Warton, 28.
Warthole, 28.
Warwick, 28.
Warrington, 24.
Wavertree, 22.
Wednesbury, 198.
Wednesday, 198.
Wellborough, 27.
Worsthorne, 37.
Wearmouth, 26.
West Derby, 23.
—— —— hundred, 5.
West Kirby, 23.
Whasset, 63.
Whithorn, 51.
—— prior of, 165.
Wigton, 62.
Wigthorpe, 62.
Wild, 64.
Wilde, 64.
Wilding, 63.
Wilbeforce, 62.
Willoughby, 62.
Willerby, 13.
Windermere, 22.
Winter Solstice, 211.
Winewall, 35.

Widdop, 36.
Wirral, 12, 24.
Whitby, 17, 26, 27.
Woollen manufacture, 64.
Worsthorne, 36.
Wulfric Spot, 24.
Wycollar, 41.
Wydale, 62.
Wylde, 10.
Wyre, 62.

Yarm, 27.
Yarborg, 84.
Yarborough, 84.
Yerburgh, 84.
Yggdrasil, 189.
Yorkshire children's folklore, 114.
Yule, origin, 211.

Zinga, 181.
Zodiac, 152.
Zoni, 181.